From the Waiting Room to the Recovery Room

By

Alma Thomas

P.O. Box 841
Tobyhanna, PA 18466
(973) 348-5067
sspublishingcompany@gmail.com
www.sharsheypublishingcompany.com

ISBN: 13: 978-0-9972668-9-4
ISBN: 10: 0-9972668-9-9
Publisher: Shar- Shey Publishing Company LLC
Book Cover Designed by: Miss Web Designer
Edited by: ATW Editing

TABLE OF CONTENTS

DEDICATION

This book is dedicated to my son, Tysean Thomas, my earthly angel. Continue to sleep in peace, my beloved. I miss you and love you with all my heart. Ms Mattie Angus, continue to sleep on. You were my inspiration to continue my education and I will never forget how you pushed me to reach for greatness.

INTRODUCTION

Timing is so important. If you are going to be successful in dance, you must be able to respond to rhythm and timing. It's the same in the Spirit. People who don't understand God's timing can become spiritually spastic, trying to make the right things happen at the wrong time. They don't get His rhythm - and everyone can tell that they are out of step. They birth things prematurely, threatening the very lives of their God-given dreams." ~ T.D Jakes

Wait for this and wait for that. The truth be told, no one really enjoys waiting, but we constantly find ourselves in a state of waiting. We spend a great deal of time in our life waiting for something. We wait for fast food, but while we are waiting it doesn't feel like it is fast. We must wait behind the car that is going slow in the fast lane and when we are tired of waiting, we will speed around them. We are always rushing from this place to that place. We wait at the railroad crossing for the train to pass. We wait at the bank and supermarket for the cashier to say 'next.' We wait for the toast to brown and the water to boil. We wait at the beauty parlor for hours to get our new do.

One of the places that causes us the most frustration is waiting in the waiting room at the doctor's office, especially when we are sick and not feeling well; we want to see the doctor and we want to see the doctor *now*. While we are in the waiting room, our patience wears thin.

We have become a society that desires instant gratification; we are a microwave generation. We want what we want and we want it immediately. Some of us are waiting for God to fulfill the promises that have been spoken in our lives and we often wonder how long before our promises are going to come to fruition.

There are times in our lives that God will place us in the waiting room. God will often use waiting to develop our character. While we are in the waiting room, there are several visitors that will stop by to visit us. The enemy will show up and sit down in the vacant seat next to us and whisper in our ear that we might as well throw in the towel. We are never going to be called out of the waiting room. We are going to die in the waiting room.

In the vacant seat on the other side of you, God has sent His angels to minister to you and they whisper in your ears that God knows that you have been waiting patiently, but you are not ready to come out of the waiting room yet. Delayed is not denied – it is a process. God is saying, "Who are you going to believe: your loving father or the father of all lies?" Delayed promises are not denied promises. Wait on them because they will come to pass.

There are times when we go to the emergency room at the hospital and, while we are waiting, they will call a person that arrived after we did and we wonder why. We might even be so bold that we voice our concern: "Why did you call them first, when I got here before they did?" The nurse will explain to us that they call in the order of emergency. We reply that they do not look like they are in any worse of a condition than we are in. We feel that our pain hurts more, our scars are deeper, but the nurse calls out 'next' and it's not you. You are still in the waiting room.

There are some valley experiences that we travel through while in the waiting room. There will be lonely times in the waiting room. People will talk about you while you are in the waiting room and they will speculate about why you are still waiting. There will be times while we are in the waiting room that we will ask God, "Why are we still waiting and people all around me are being called out of the waiting room?" We wonder if God has forgotten that we are still waiting. Did God call my name and I didn't hear Him, or did I miss my divine appointment?

In this book, I want you to come and wait with me in the waiting room. I want to share with you how I made it personally from the waiting room to the operating room to the delivery room. How God turned my pain into purpose. It is my prayer as I share my thoughts and feelings with you that somebody will come out of their waiting room and step into their destiny.

My waiting room experience started on February 13, 2009 in the emergency room at the Mid Island Hospital in Levittown New York. That night started like any other night with me saying goodnight to my children and going to bed. I woke up at 2:00 in the morning and my son asked me if I was going into the kitchen. I asked him why and he said, "Because I want some water." I gave him the water that I had in my hand and then he said, "Mommy, I don't feel well. I need to go to the hospital."

I called an ambulance. He was talking all the way into the ambulance, but when we got to the hospital they were performing CPR on him. They took him in the back and later the doctor came and got me. He said the words that I never want to hear again: "We did all we could do. We couldn't save him."

It was on that day that my waiting room experience began and it would last for five long years. On December 31, 2013 I was finally called from the waiting room to the operating room to the delivery room.

Sometimes when we are waiting on God to speak, He's waiting for us to listen. ~ Martha Bolton.

I think I hear my name being called. It is time for my examination. I need to tell them who I am and what my issues are.

CHAPTER ONE

Who do you think you are?

For as he thinketh in his heart, so is he. Eat and drink saith he to thee, but his heart is not with thee. ~ Proverbs 23:7

It is when we face the most difficult times of our lives that we discover who we are and exactly what we are made of. The truth is, whatever we think about on a continual basis will become what is engraved in our hearts. What or who you think you are has a huge impact on what you will become. The more that you dwell on something – positive or negative – the more of an impact that thing will have in your life. If you are already defeated in your mind, then you will lose the will to fight.

While you are in the waiting room, it is your mindset that needs to be transformed for you to survive the waiting room experience. The devil will feed you lies that your present situation has been predestined by your past mistakes and failures. While I was in the waiting room, the devil was my constant companion. He made visits during visiting hours and in the midnight hours. It was during these visits that he spoke to me and tried to convince me that my waiting room experience was never going to end and that I deserved what I was going through. I tried not to internalize the devil's lies, but it was hard not to listen to him.

While you are in the waiting room, the more that you entertain the devil and the more you send out invitations to your pity party, the more you dance with the devil and the more he will zap the life out of you.

There are many lessons that I learned while I was in the waiting room. One of the most important is that you cannot share your dreams, aspirations, and visions with everyone. You will be shocked to know that even those people that you feel should be praying for you are praying against you and waiting for you to fail. They do not want you to ever leave the waiting room.

Because of your vulnerable and weakened state, the devil desires to kill you while you are in the waiting room. He wants to make sure that you never make it to the delivery room. The enemy strategically places dream killers in your camp. They will tell you that those things that you desire are out of your reach.

I learned the hard way that everybody that you call friend doesn't desire the best for you. While I was in the waiting room, I learned that sometimes it's best to be silent and let your conversations be between you and God. There are some things that you must keep to yourself.

There are times in our lives when we must plant in secret and water them in the midnight hour with our tears. When it is time to sow, only God will be able to get the glory. In my weakest hour, I had to realize that God doesn't make a mistake and that no matter what it looked like and no matter what it felt like now, God still had a plan for my life. It was while I was in the waiting room that I had to remind myself of the Word of God and to remind myself of His Word.

Before I formed thee in the belly I knew thee; and before thou camest forth out of the womb I sanctified thee, and I ordained thee a prophet unto the nations ~ Jeremiah 1:5

The prophet Jeremiah, as well as you and I, was born foreknown to God and we have been set apart for the master's use.

It is while we are in the waiting room that we must understand that during our waiting room experience, God is our charge nurse and He is carefully watching over us and charting our progress. Our very existence, every pain, every disappointment, every heartache was a reality while we were still in our mother's womb. Sometimes during life's fiercest storms we must be reminded that God formed us for a purpose and that there is nothing that is hidden from God.

From our birth, God knew that we were going to make mistakes and that we would suffer broken hearts that would rock us to our very core. There would be times that we would feel like we could not make it – that we weren't going to make it. He knew that we would suffer some loses that would leave us devastated. He knew that even in our hours of desperation, we would mess up time after time. It is during these times that He is whispering, "My child, don't be dismayed. I knew that you were going to mess up. I know that you failed the test, but I love you so I am going to let you take the test again. I am the God of the do-over. If you have a repentant heart, I will allow you to do it repeatedly."

But now thus saith the Lord that created thee: O Jacob and he that formed thee. O Israel: Fear not for I have redeemed thee. I have called you by thy name; thou art mine. When thou passed through the waters, I will be with thee; and through the rivers, they shall not overflow; when thou walks through the fire, thou shalt not be burned; neither shall thou flame kindle upon thee. ~ Isaiah 43:1-2

What God is saying to you, beloved, is that "I created you and I called you out by your name. Nothing is hidden from me and no matter what you go through in life, I got your back. I made you with all your imperfections and I love you in spite of it all."

It is while you are in the waiting room that you begin to question who you are. It is the lies of the enemy that make us think less of ourselves. While you are in the waiting room, the enemy will set you up to believe that you are never going to make it out. The Bible provides us with so many examples of people who God placed in the waiting room. They waited for years for God's promises to be fulfilled in their life, and while they were waiting, they suffered many things. Most people do not like to wait, but the Bible gives us many examples of people who waited on the Lord. Mary and Martha waited on Jesus to come and heal their brother who was sick and when Jesus got there, he was dead. They said that Jesus was too late, but he was right on time to call Lazarus out of the grave. Abraham waited on the promises of God. Noah waited for the rain. Daniel waited on the Lord to deliver him out of the lion's den and the three Hebrew boys waited in the fiery furnace. One highly regarded example is Joseph. Joseph's brother tried to abort his destiny.

Another lesson that I learned in the waiting room was from Joseph's life. That lesson is that your haters will only hate on your dream when they realize that your dream will come to pass, that one day you will be released from your waiting room into your purpose, and that your dreams will be manifested in time. I told you earlier that there are times when you need to keep your dreams a secret especially when you are doubtful. But when you realize who you are, it doesn't matter that you are in your waiting season right now; you know without a shadow of a doubt that God is going to bring you out.

It is during this time that you need to speak your dreams into the spiritual realm so they can be manifested in the natural realm. Joseph's brother realized that there was something different about Joseph. That was why hated Joseph. It had nothing to do with his coat, but what that coat represented which was the anointing on his life. It is not you that people are hating on, but it is the anointing that is over your life. Joseph's brothers were trying to destroy the anointing that Joseph had so they put him in a pit and then sold him into slavery thinking that was the end of him and his dreams. But I am writing this book to let somebody know right now in chapter one that no matter how long you are in the waiting room, can't no devil in hell stop what God has for you.

I need for you to understand what is happening right now in Joseph's life. The favorite son has now become a slave. He went from riches to rags. He was betrayed and abandoned by his own family, a family that per our society's standards would be considered dysfunctional. Even in those dire circumstances, he rose in prominence and found favor with the king. We would think that right now Joseph was living in his purpose, but we would soon find out that Joseph was still in his waiting room experience, that God will continue to bless even while we are waiting. Soon Joseph would be placed in a difficult situation. The king's wife develops an attraction to Joseph and wanted him to have an affair with her. The devil will send you what he thinks you like in a pretty package, but Joseph refused to take what the devil was offering and that landed him in jail. We don't know how long Joseph was in jail, but we know that he arrived in Egypt when he was seventeen, and he was about thirty when he was released from prison.

I am sure that while Joseph sits and contemplates what God has shown him and the reality of what is happening in his life right now, there were several responses that Joseph could have had while he was sitting in God's waiting room. The first one is anger. When things happen in our lives that we feel like we don't deserve, oftentimes we will get angry. Sometimes we feel bitterness because we try to do what we feel is our best, and bad things still happen to us. We wonder, "Why me?"

Joseph could have been mad at Potiphar and his wife. Everything that Joseph stood for was in question: his character, his integrity, even his faith in God was in question, but Joseph refused to compromise. Even in jail, God favored Joseph. Joseph did not try to manipulate the situation while he was in the waiting room – he waited on God. He could have slandered the king's name and said, "After all that I've done for him, he believed his lying wife and not me." But Joseph did not sink to such low levels. He did not fall and he did not bend, even though they were whispering about him and telling lies on him. He held on to his integrity. Joseph realized, even in his prison waiting room, who he was in God. So he waited on God to fulfill the promises in his life. While he was waiting, he wasn't just sitting in his prison cell feeling sorry for himself. He worked while he was in prison, again rising to a position of favor in the jail. He continued speaking of the goodness of God and he continued to seek God's face.

Sometimes when we are in the waiting room, we began to lose focus and to take our eyes off God. We look with our natural eyes at our present situations and lose sight of where God is trying to take us. We must realize that even in our waiting rooms, we have the power to tap into God's favor. But when we do not realize who we are during the waiting room process, we will begin to forsake our former dreams. While you are in the waiting room, you will gently begin to rock your dreams to sleep.

When you know who you are, you will understand that even in your waiting room, God does not leave you alone to wait, but that He is with you. Sometimes this realization is a process because sometimes, because of our past mistakes and failures, we do not know where we stand with God. We don't know how much we mean to God and thereby we suffer from identity crisis.

From the pit to the palace, to the prison and back to the palace, Joseph always understood who he was to God. He believed with his whole heart in the Scripture that God had promised his father Jacob. We understand that Jacob was far from perfect, but God still had a covenant with him and Joseph held on to this Scripture:

> *And, behold, I am with thee, and will keep thee in all places whither thou goest, and will bring thee again into this land; for I will not leave thee, until I have done that which I have spoken to thee of. ~ Genesis 28:15*

God is saying here that no matter where you go, He is going to be with you and that He is going to keep you until His promises over your life are fulfilled. Somebody should be shouting right now as they are reading this book because God isn't finished with you yet! Even while you are sitting in the waiting room, you are never alone because God Himself has promised never to leave you. The enemy may come and try to distract you from what God has promised you. The enemy might even try to whisper in your ear that you will never achieve the dreams, visions, and aspiration that God has placed in your belly.

What we need to learn from Joseph is that no matter what it looks like or what it feels like, God longs for us to realize who we are in Him and what He desires for our life. Every one of us has a purpose for our lives and we are not here on earth just to be here. The first step of our purpose begins with us knowing who we are in God. We must realize that even in our waiting stages, God has a plan for our lives. But often in our waiting rooms we allow the enemy to frustrate our purpose. The enemy is holding us captive in our mind. We come to church with our defenses up, and instead of holding up holy hands, we have allowed the enemy to steal our identity; we are a victim of identity theft. The enemy has hacked your life.

We must understand the greater the conquest, the greater the battle that you must fight. It is time that you take your identity back and realize who you are. Some of us have had amnesia far too long and if we don't realize who we are, quick dementia will set in. It is time to know who we are in Christ. While we are in the waiting room, we need to activate whatever we need to get us to the next level in God.

It is time, my beloveds, for us to envision ourselves as God sees us. He does not see us as who we are now, but He sees us as we are going to be. For us to know who we are in Christ, we need to deal with those issues that keep us in the waiting room.

Remember the doors are not made of unbreakable steel, but they are still locked. So let's deal with our issues that keep us in the waiting room.

CHAPTER TWO

What are your issues?

Keep thy heart with all diligence; for out of it are the issues of life. ~ Proverbs 4:23

Everybody has problems. We understand that problems are an everyday part of life. We face problems in our home, work and in society. But when those problems become so overwhelming that they begin to affect every part of your daily existence, you no longer have just an ordinary problem, you now have an issue. These issues seem to intensify while we are in the waiting seasons of our life. These issues appear larger than life in our waiting room. Many of the issues that we must deal with while sitting in the waiting room are those that have deep roots. Some are planted deep in our childhood.

Many of us laugh and make jokes when people go to the psychologist and the first thing that he tells us is to lie down on the couch and tell him about our childhood. Sometimes when we want to kill our issues from the root, we might have to go to Doctor Jesus and tell him about our childhood.

The truth is that these unresolved issues are the ones that are going to resurface during our waiting room experience. Our life's experiences and how we dealt with them have shaped us into who we are today. Our reaction to our background is what either makes us resilient and able to rise above our circumstances, or on the flip side, it's what makes us bitter and makes us plan our present circumstances based on past mistakes.

While we are in the waiting room, we allow our tests, trials, and struggles to make us acrimonious.

There is a cliché that says, "When life gives us lemons we should make lemonade," but we need to know just how to make lemons into lemonade. Lemons do not just become lemonade – we must take a bitter situation and make it sweet. We must learn how to play the hand that God gives us. We cannot just throw our hands up; it can mean the difference between success and failure. Lingering in the waiting room or getting out.

There are countless different types of issues: emotional, physical, financial and spiritual just to name a few. These various types of issues can have a lingering effect on us while we are in the waiting room, and we need to examine our lives to see what impact these issues have had on us.

Emotional issues can lead to stagnation in our lives. For example, if we as children did not receive the love that we needed growing up, then a vital part of our life is left with a void. We always feel like we are missing a piece to our puzzle and a puzzle that is missing one piece is not any good. As adults, we tend to search for that love in all the wrong places. We might search for love in food, sex, alcohol, drugs, or in the arms of a person who doesn't really love us. There is a secular song (I hope that none of the church people who are reading this book are too deep for this), but there is a song by Candi Stanton, "Young Hearts Run Free," and the words to the song say:

> *Young hearts to yourself be true. Don't be no fool when love really don't love you. You will count up years and they will be filled with tears.*

In my life, when I was looking for love in all the wrong places, I would go to the bar and the party looking for Mr. Goodbar, and time and time again I would come home with a Snickers or a Three Musketeers, but never Mr. Right. Sometimes it was Mr. Right Now.

Sometimes you will feel like you are unworthy of God's love, when you read John 3:16 that says:

For God so loved the world that he gave his only begotten son that whoever believes in him should not perish, but have everlasting life.

But sometimes in our waiting room we ask God, "Even me? You cannot mean me. I am unlovable. My daddy walked away and didn't love me. Life allowed some horrible things to happen to me. There are some things that I survived that nobody but God and I know about. There are so many skeletons in my closet, God, even you can't love me. I am so dirty. I want to be clean of these feelings, but truth be told, I just do not know how." You often say, "God, you cannot love me because right now I do not even love myself."

When you do not love yourself, you are not in any position for anyone else to love you. You only set yourself up for disappointment when you look to others to validate and love you. Many women suffer from low self-esteem and we paint on a phony smile that says everything is all right with me. We pretend that we are all that and a bag of chips, but beneath all of that is just a bag of crumbs. Beneath our tough girl exterior is a little insecure girl who is hiding in the corners of our heart. We never allowed that little girl to grow up; we stunted her growth and then hid her from the public eye. It is time that we minister to our young girls and women and instill in them that they are a diamond and a pearl and they are more than boobs and butt, to put it mildly. Their value is not between their thighs.

Some women do not know their worth and they attach themselves to unhealthy relationships. Each time they enter a new relationship they expect things to be different, but they pick men with the same mentality as the last one. Truth be told, men are like dogs and they can sniff out when you are vulnerable. They are dealing with their own issues and we are trying to love each other while neither one of us have been healed.

In my pursuit of love, I attached myself to men who did not who they were, so how could they value me? We are somebody in the sight of God. He says in His Word:

> *I will praise thee, for I am fearfully and wonderfully made: marvelous are thy works; and that my soul knoweth right well. ~ Psalm 139:14*

God speaks to our self-image. In His Word, He declares that we are wonderfully made. With all of my curves, God made me and I am beautiful in His sight. But unfortunately, many of us do not feel that we are beautiful and that we are precious in the sight of God. These emotional issues of worthlessness, low self-esteem, lack of self-confidence, and discouragement cannot just be wished away.

If we do not deal with these issues, they will resurface again and again in different stages of our lives. These issues will especially show up in your waiting room experience.

As I am writing this book right now, I feel the spirit of release. I am releasing some issues and some people from my past. I forgive everybody who ever hurt me. I forgive the children on the playground that called me fat and did not let me play any games. I release the children who called me throw up girl because I threw up once in the third grade. I release everybody that laughed at me because I could not afford the latest clothes. I forgive every man who ever cheated on me and told me that they loved me, but knew that they did not. I forgive everybody that ever lied on me and scandalized my name. I forgive my daddy for not being there and I forgive myself for the things that I did when I did not love myself.

I realize now that because of some of my unresolved emotional issues, I have aligned myself with many unhealthy relationships over the years. There have been times in my life that I did not feel like I was worthy of anything better.

When others are going through their waiting room experience, I can encourage them. I can proclaim to them that they are coming out of whatever situation they are in. But when it comes to me achieving my dreams, aspirations, and visions, I have placed God in a box in my life. It is time that I take off my mask. Underneath this smile, I was battling issues of discouragement, depression, oppression, and even suicidal thoughts. And while I was in the waiting room, many of my issues resurfaced.

In recent months, there has been an increase in pastors and church people committing suicide. It is sad that we hide behind our positions and titles and what we think people are going to say when they find out that we are an emotional wreck. So, instead, we hide and we are literally dying. I thank God that He spoke to me in my waiting room and said that I shall live and not die and declare the works of the Lord.

As a church, we are not doing enough to deal with the emotional issues that are hiding in our pews every Sunday. We try to minister to the spirit without dealing with the emotional issues, scars, and the residue that remain in our lives. Many of us come to church battered and bruised and abused. The leaders in the church will put a bandage on the wound. The wound is rotting and stinking underneath. Some of us cannot deal with the emotional issues of others because we are still dealing with our issues.

As we learned earlier, unresolved problems become issues, and now issues that are unresolved will become strongholds in our lives.

> *For the weapons of our warfare are not carnal but mighty through God to the pulling down of strongholds. Casting down imaginations and every high thing that exalted itself against the knowledge of God, and bringing into captivity every thought to the obedience of Christ. ~ 2 Corinthians10; 4-5*

It was while I was in the waiting room that I realized that even though I had been saved for years, I had not experienced true deliverance because I had these strongholds in my life. There is a process that we must go through to pull down or to destroy these strongholds. If we allow these nuisances to survive, then our past can hinder our future. There is no way that we can go back and relive our past; there is no way to go back and erase all the failures and mistakes that you made in the past. The only way that you can really heal is to face your past head on and to move on. In my waiting room experience, I came to grips with the painful fact that my past was keeping me from enjoying the present and looking forward to the future.

It is my sincerest prayer that as you are reading this book, you are not just turning the pages of yet another inspirational book, but you are reading it with expectancy for a change in your condition. A change in your emotional, physical, and spiritual state of mind. A change in your mindset and your way of thinking.

When your past is filled with overwhelming pain, it impedes your ability to move forward. It is important that we move forward because if we hold on to our past, we will continue to sabotage our relationships – even our relationship with Christ. It is okay to release the pain of your past, your secret shame, and to finally expose the skeletons in your life that want to fall out of the closet. You do not have to remain in an emotional prison because of your past. Your past doesn't have to determine your future.

In my waiting room, I found out that I was stinking and decaying because I had not deal with the issues of my past. To experience healing, I had to pull off the bandage, and when pulled off the bandage, it hurt. It hurt like hell, but it was necessary for me to pull it off for me to step into my destiny. I finally had to deal with my issues, and for healing to occur in your life, you must deal with your issues. It is time to identity your issue and kill it before it kills you.

The Bible has many examples of people who have gone through similar situations to the ones that we face today. In the Bible, there is a woman who had emotional, physical, and spiritual issues. For this woman to crawl into her destiny, she had to deal with her issues. In the Bible, this woman is only identified as the woman with the issue of blood. We do not know her name; her name is not important, but what is important is that she had an issue.

> *And a woman having an issue twelve years, which had spent all her living upon physicians, neither could be healed of any. ~ Luke 8:43*

How many of us have tried everything before we came to God? For twelve years, this woman had tried all other solutions. She had spent her very last penny on doctors. This woman suffered for twelve long years. Many of us women cannot even imagine that; most of us go through three to five days and that is too much for us. The doctors tried remedy after remedy, but nothing could ease her suffering and pain. For twelve years, she had been forsaken by men. She suffered loneliness and low self-esteem. As we know from the book of Leviticus, she was considered unclean, therefore no man would come near her. Her own family had ostracized her.

While I was in my waiting room, I could feel what the woman with the issue of blood was feeling because at certain points during my waiting process, I felt like I was all alone and hurting. Per the Scriptures, she had a discharge of blood. She was scorned and labeled unclean. Even the very bed that she laid on was contaminated. This nameless woman had expended all that she had just because she desired to be unpolluted. She knew that she was dirty, but she desperately wanted to be clean. The woman's physical condition was that she was hemorrhaging blood. The loss of blood caused her to be feeble and weak.

If you would just allow me to use my spiritual imagination… Day after day, she could barely lift her frail and ailing body off that fouled, dirty, defiled bed. When she was finally able to drag her afflicted body out of the bed, she went about her daily business, alone and isolated. This loneliness and the effect that her illness had on her, led to her not only having physical issues, but she was also suffering from emotional issues. She had no one to say I love you. There wasn't anybody to say everything is going to be all right. There wasn't anyone to encourage her. There wasn't anyone to speak to her issue and say, "It is already done, you will be healed in the name of Jesus."

How many times have we found ourselves all alone? Sometimes we are surrounded by people, but still feel like we are alone. There are points in our lives when we face obstacles and we must suffer alone. The Bible doesn't specifically tell us if she had a husband or children, but we can decipher from the circumstances that if she ever had a family, they had disappeared a long time ago. After all, how long will a man stay when he cannot hold his wife in his arms and she is not able to fulfill her wifely duties?

When a man hath taken a wife, and married her, and it come to pass that she finds no favor in his eyes, because he hath found some uncleanness in her: then let him write her a bill of divorcement, and give it in her hand, and send her out of his house. ~ Deuteronomy 24:1

She couldn't even rock her own babies to sleep. She wasn't allowed to attend a place of worship. She wasn't allowed to lift holy hands with the other saints. She couldn't approach the throne of grace. She couldn't attend the weekly services. The missionary wasn't visiting her to see if she needed anything. She was in a downward spiral. She was dying spiritually. This woman's constant hemorrhaging was a calamity. This issue had left her weak and barely able to walk. Financially, she had spent all that she had. She had no money and was unable to take care of her basic needs. She was ceremonially unclean. She was searching for a cure, but a cure could not be found

But one day, she heard about a man named Jesus and, somehow, she had heard that Jesus was a healer. She heard that this man called Jesus had opened blind eyes and caused deaf ears to hear. The lame had come to him crawling, but left leaping and jumping. Demons were cast back into the pits of hell from whence they came. Perhaps she had heard that Jairus, an officer in the synagogue, had called Jesus to heal his daughter who was dead. Perhaps she had sat all alone at her window and heard the people worshipping and praising this man called Jesus who was a miracle worker. In her waiting room situation, she somehow received the news; she had not been in service for twelve long years. I am confident that in her years of waiting all alone and praying for some release, that sometimes she had to encourage herself like David:

> *And David was greatly distressed for the people spake of stoning him, because the soul of all the people was grieved, every man for his sons and daughters, but David encouraged himself in the Lord his God. ~ 1 Samuel 36:6*

She had to encourage herself because there was no one there to tell her that she was going to make it. Even though the woman had been in her waiting room for over twelve years, she still had enough faith to believe that if she could just make it to Jesus, all her issues would be healed; her stronghold would be pulled down. For her to get to Jesus, she had to break religious laws and traditions. The laws said that she could not be around people, and laws would not allow her within ten feet of Jesus, so there would be no way that she would have been allowed to touch him. But she was desperate and she could not allow people's opinions of her to stop her. She could not allow religious folks or legalism to keep her in this weak, crippled state.

How many times do we allow what people think of us to keep us from our blessings? At one time in my life, I was in a backslidden state. I was harboring hate and unforgiveness in my heart. I was in mental bondage, spending many sleepless nights thinking about all of the people who had hurt me and done me wrong in my life. I got to the place where I was hurting so bad that I could not do what God had called me to do. I was ministering out of a place of hurt.

One Sunday morning, I so desperately wanted to be free in my mind. I could hear the song break every chain and I started to cry out to God that I wanted to be free. I wanted the chains to be broken off of my life. I had finally realized that my marriage was over, that it never had a chance because I made a permanent decision while I was still in my waiting room, which was a temporary situation. I was so desperate to be free that I did not care what the church folks thought of me standing at the altar sobbing and crying, because I needed a touch from the master.

Just like the woman with the issue of blood. She pushed her way through the crowd. She was so weak and feeble that she could not run to Jesus. She could not even walk. Oh, I can picture her. The image is so vivid. She was sitting there in her waiting room, contemplating what her next move would be. What she did know was that she was sick and tired of being sick; she was tired of being alone; tired of being dirty and unclean. For twelve long years, she had no human interaction, but she was positive that her wait would be over if she could somehow get to Jesus. If she could just touch the hem of his garment, then she knew that she would be made whole.

On that one fateful day, she decided that today would be the day that she would be liberated, so she made her way through the crowd. She was so weak and so feeble that no one even noticed her. She had changed so much in the last twelve years that she did not look familiar to anyone, so she reached out for Jesus. She was dirty and broken. All that she could grab hold of was a simple piece of his garment, but as soon as she touched him, she realized that her life would be forever changed, for immediately, the blood stopped flowing. That nasty blood that for twelve years had ruined her life, suddenly stopped flowing.

The master felt that life-changing moment when the healing virtue emanated from his body and it had not returned unto him void, but it had accomplished what it had set out to do.

The master knew that somebody's wait was over, that someone's life was forever changed, because you cannot come into contact with the master and your life not be changed. The woman with the issue of blood, the nameless woman, her wait was finally over, but she was still afraid. She was healed, but she was still broken. The fear stemmed from years of unresolved issues, the years of being physically sick, emotionally drained, spiritually dead, and financially broke – all issues that take a toll on you. It causes stress and depression.

Many of us have been living with our issues for years and these issues have us all dressed up on the outside, but inside our issues are tearing us apart. These issues have made some of us angry and confused. Some of us are suffering from anxiety and depression. I suffered with anxiety and panic attacks for many years. Many of us live with emotional pain that we hide from the world. We have suffered at the hands of others because of our past pains and hurts. We, like the woman with the issue of blood, have tried to fix our issues on our own after we have tried all the methods of the world. But the more that we try, the worse the issues seem to get.

It is time for us to finally rid ourselves of these physical, spiritual, emotional, and financial issues that have kept us chained to our past instead of cherishing our present and looking forward to our future. It is time for us to reach for the master's garment and get a touch – all we need is a touch from the master. It will not be easy and it will be a major battle. It is right now that you must decide that you are ready for battle, but before you can fight effectively, you must recognize the weapons of the enemy.

CHAPTER THREE

Recognizing the enemy

No weapon that is formed against thee shall prosper; and every tongue that shall rise against thee in judgment thou shalt condemn. ~ Isaiah 54:17

There is a constant battle that goes on in our minds. There is a war going on and many of our Christian soldiers are becoming casualties of war. Many of our fallen soldiers were not prepared for the war and many did not realize that there was even a war going on. They did not recognize the enemy or the weapons that are in the enemy's arsenal. Therefore, it is important that we realize that we are in a war. We must understand who our enemy is and be able to recognize his weapons of mass destruction. It is important to identify the fiery darts that he will fire our way.

One of the major weapons that he will use is deception and confusion. He will have us so confused that we do not know who our real enemy is. The devil will use many strategies to win the war and he has declared war on all Christians. Satan is scheming and conniving. He will attempt to twist the very Word of the Lord. He has been waging war since the Garden of Eden when he discovered Eve with the forbidden fruit.

For God doth know the day ye eat, thereof, then your eyes shall be opened and ye shall be as gods, knowing good and evil. And when the woman saw that the tree was good for food and that it was pleasant to the eyes, and a tree to be desired to make one wise, she took of the fruit thereof and did eat and gave also unto her husband with her and he did eat. ~ Genesis 5:6

The woman looked and saw that the tree was good to eat and it appealed to her appetite. Satan tempted Eve with all the things that concerned her thoughts and her mind. He made it appealing to her desires and her free will. He tempted Eve with the forbidden fruit and likewise today, he is still tempting us with those things that are forbidden by the laws of God. He is constantly dangling these things in front of us so there is a war within our flesh. He will make these forbidden things look like fun and make us feel like we are missing something.

Satan appeals to man's senses and tempts us with those things that feel good. He will tempt you with fornication, drugs, alcohol, and sex. Once you get addicted to these things they will become strongholds in your life. The drug addict did not just wake up one day and declare to their parents, "I want to be a drug addict when I grow up." What happens is that they make one bad choice after another until their problems become an issue. Satan is an expert at what he does and he realizes that man does not want to deny himself. So, Satan makes you believe that these pleasures of the world will lead to happiness, and for years, you chase that happiness that always seems to evade you.

Another weapon in Satan's arsenal is doubt. Doubt is the uneasiness that we feel and the uncertainties that we face in life. Doubt is also a lack of faith and trust. Satan will make you doubt your abilities, visions, and aspirations. Satan will attempt to make you doubt the Word of God and the promises that God has for your life. If you are doubting the Word of God, you will never possess the power that God says that you have in Him.

> *For verily I say unto you that whosoever shall say unto this mountain, be thou removed and cast into the sea, and shall not doubt in his heart, but shall believe these things which he saith shall come to pass; he shall have whatsoever he saith. ~ Mark 11:23*

Doubt is one of Satan's chief weapons because if he can cause you to doubt in your mind, then he has already won the battle. He will make you believe that you are never coming out of the waiting room and you will be struggling with the same issues year after year. The woman with the issue of blood would have died of her illness if she had doubted that Jesus was able to heal her. Satan uses our past to penetrate the doubts into our very soul. Satan will capitalize on the fact that we feel unworthy of God's love and he will make us question that even Jesus could love us.

For God so loved the world that he sent his only begotten son that whosoever shall believe in him shall not perish. ~ John 3:16

The Word of God says that we have only to believe, but the enemy will make you skeptical that these words include you. You will find yourself in moments of doubt whispering, "Even me, Lord? Even me? Because I am not worthy of your love. You don't know where I have been. You do not know what I have done. You don't even know the thoughts that I have thought." I know that the Word says *whosoever* and that whosoever includes even me.

God knew us even before we were conceived in our mother's womb and He knew that we were going to make mistakes repeatedly. He even knew that I, one day, would even doubt His love for me. Satan doesn't want you to know that you are a part of God's salvation plan, because if you could only internalize that, then you will no longer doubt God's Word and His plan for your life. And you would render one of Satan's weapons ineffective.

Satan is a liar. As a matter of fact, he is the father of all lies. He does not want you to believe the truth because he knows that the truth will set you free, and you can be set free from those issues that have kept you locked in bondage. Satan realizes that only the truth can set you free. We declare it all the time that the truth will set you free – we sing it, we put it on banners, but do we really believe it? The reality of it all is that the truth is the only thing that can act as a wire cutter and cut those shackles off your feet.

And you shall know the truth and the truth shall make you free ~ Mark 8:32

Another weapon in Satan's arsenal is fear. He will use our fears to hold us hostage. We have all, at one time or another in our life, come face to face with fear. We are afraid that the things that happened in our past will resurface. We are afraid of flying or the dark, just to name a few things that we fear. Fear limits you and will stop you from doing certain things. Satan has one purpose and that purpose is to destroy and devour you. Fear is a prison; it will cripple and stagnate you. Fear will stop you and it will prevent you from having what God has for you. Satan will use fear to hold our thoughts hostage. If the woman with the issue of blood had allowed the fear of tradition to keep her home that one fateful day, she never would have come into contact with the Healer and the Deliverer.

There are so many fears. One of the main fears that Satan uses is the fear of failure because after all, we like a winner. In the world of sports, if a team starts having a losing streak, then ticket sales will plummet. We teach children at an early age to strive to win because we like winners, not failures. We do not want the word 'failure' associated with our name so, at times, we won't even try because we do not want to fail.

I can accept failure, everyone fails at something. But I can't accept not trying. ~ Michael Jordan

Failure is a part of life.

For all have sinned and come short of the glory of God" ~ Romans 3:23

Everyone fails at some point. We all make mistakes. Many of us have fallen short and during these times we feel embarrassed. The devil will tell you that you are in this condition because you are not worthy and that failure is your destiny, that you can read all the self-help books that you want. Yes, it is true that when we fall, God wants us to feel convicted, but not condemned. But the enemy wants to make our issues look so bad that we think that even God will not forgive us. The fear of failure is so much greater than the actual failure because if you try and fail, you can try again. But if you are so afraid that you will not even try, then you are already defeated and you will never accomplish your purpose in life.

The fear of failure haunts you night after night. If the woman with the issue of blood had given up after going to doctor after doctor and still there was no cure to be found, she would have missed her blessing. I am sure that the enemy spoke to her mind and told her that it was over. She realized that the difference between successful people and people who fail is that people who fail simply give up, while the people who succeed are those who do not quit. They refuse to allow their issues to keep them down. The woman with the issue of blood did not listen to the enemy when he told her to just lie down and bleed to death. But she was persistent, determined, and had endurance.

The devil is laughing when we allow our fears to take over our minds. He is rejoicing because he knows that he has won a major battle. It is fear that makes our faith weak. Fear will make our lives unproductive and ineffective. Failure is not failing to reach your dreams – failure is never having a dream. The fear of failure will rob us of our goals, visions, and aspirations. Fear will keep us in our comfort zone. Fear says, "I am not even going to try because I know that I am not going to make it." Most of the fears that we experience are not even real, but the devil knows that fear is a powerful weapon because fear will stunt your growth. Fear will keep us from enjoying what God has planned for us.

Another weapon that the enemy uses is our past. He will use our past mistakes and failures to keep us in mental bondage. There are issues from our childhood that the enemy will continually throw in our face. He will tell us that we were cursed from the womb. As you sit in the waiting room of life, he will whisper sweet nothings in your ear. He will tell you that you are the offspring of a loser; therefore, you are destined to be a loser. If your parents were addicted to alcohol or drugs then he will tell you that is your fate as well. You are predestined to be an addict. If your parents were uneducated, then you might as well rock your dream to sleep, that you cannot be a doctor because you are not a Huxtable. He will tell you that greatness is not in your future.

These haunting words often speak to the insecure little girl inside of you. These words from the enemy will keep you in a mental prison. You are too afraid to even come to the fight because the skeletons might fall out of your closet, and you feel like you have already lost the battle. But I am writing this book to expose the devil as the liar that he is. As I am writing this book, I am in a battle with him. He did not want me to write this book; I have been writing this book for over seven years now. He is telling me to put away my pen because no one wants to hear the story of a loser like me. He thought I was still that insecure little girl with the nappy hair and the hand me down clothes.

> *That which has been is now and that which is to be have already been and God requires that which is past. ~ Ecclesiastes 3:15*

God wants an account of our past for our benefit. It is meant to make us better, not bitter. He wants us to be able to look back over our lives and see what He has already done for us. There's a song that says: if He does not do anything else for us, He has done enough already. When we look back over our lives, we can see the times that God has delivered us out of situations. But the enemy will try to distort that picture and he will continually replay scenes from our lives. He will show us those times from our past when we were ashamed, or our issues of depression and loneliness. He wants us to believe that with all our issues, God will not be able to use someone like us. No, we are not worth God's blessings because our lives are such a mess.

Satan will also use the weapon of lies and deception. He will make those things that are not real appear as if they are real. He will tell you that you are sick and you will never get well. He will tell you that you are crazy and that there is no God. He will whisper in your ear that you are a nobody and God could never use a nobody like you. But I am so glad that God, even with all my issues, went into the junkyard and he went into the dumpster and found me almost dead and stinking from all my issues. He cleaned me up and made me a vessel. A living testimony that God is willing and able to use – and will use you – no matter what your issues are. God has a big investment in our lives and it is His desire to see us be all that He designed us to be. God will tell

Satan to back off and *touch not my anointed and do my prophets no harm. ~ 1Chronicles 16:22*

God is concerned about every aspect of our lives, but the enemy will try and cloud our vision, so while we are in the waiting room, we do not see this. Satan's weapons are only effective against us because we have allowed his fiery darts to become embedded in our thoughts and they have taken up roots in our lives.

Verily, verily I say onto you. Except acorn of wheat fall into the ground and die, it abideth alone: but if it die, it bringeth forth much fruit. ~ John 12:24

We are that fertile ground that God is referring to. Our shallow ground has been broken up by our pain, heartaches, and disappointments and it has been developed by our mistakes and failures. In the midnight hour when we are all alone, we will water them with our tears. God has placed something special deep inside of us and that is why we are on Satan's assassination list. He realizes our potential, sometimes even before we do. What we need to understand is that even in our darkest hour, it was God's great concern that kept us standing. Even the strongest of soldiers would fall down if they went through just half of what we have already gone through – and we are still standing.

> *But he knoweth the way that I take and when he has tried me, I shall come forth as true gold. ~ Job 23:10*

There is a saying that when the going gets tough, the tough gets going. There will be a time in every believer's life when our life, like Job's, will take a turn for the worse. It is during these times that the enemy will make us feel that God has forgotten us, or that we are so bad that God does not love us. We also have to remember that it is not always the enemy, but sometimes it is us, and we need to stop sabotaging our own lives. God knows all about us. He knows all of our thoughts and actions and the situations that we will encounter even before we go through them. He knows your past, your present, and your future.

Fire is used to refine gold – that means to make it better. Before my waiting room experience, I felt like God had placed greatness in my life. But during my waiting room experience, I felt like God had forgotten all about me. My future appeared bleak and I had to muster enough faith to wait on God. As He placed me in the waiting room, I had to learn that fire does not burn gold, it purifiers it. You might be going through the fire, but it is only to make you stronger. When you want a cup of tea, the stronger you want the tea, the longer you let the teabag stay in the hot water. The stronger that God wants you, the longer He allows you to sit in the waiting room.

We have to realize that fiction is one of the strongest weapons that the enemy will ever use on us because, if in this battle he can conquer our thoughts and hold them hostage as a prisoner of war, then he has wounded us and left us to die. If the enemy can control our thoughts – the ones that we hide behind phony smiles, masks, and walls of insecurity – and keep us revisiting those negative thoughts from our past, then he controls us. The saddest part is that we do not recognize who the enemy is or what his weapons of mass destruction are. If we do not recognize the enemy and understand how he works in our lives, then the results will be a disaster.

It is time to pinpoint who the enemy is and what weapons he has already imposed in our lives. For the Word of God lets us know that He has weapons:

> *No weapon that is formed against thee shall prosper and every tongue that shall rise against thee in judgment thou shall condemn ~ Isaiah 54:17*

Our enemies have boasted that they are going to take us down. But what we have to realize is that even when we are in the waiting room, the fight is fixed. When God is on your side, who can be against you?

Yes the enemy will form his weapons, but the Word of God says that these weapons will not prosper. It is your choice today – you can choose to allow the enemy to continue to bomb your mind with his weapons of mass destruction, or you can decide that it is time for you to have victory in your life.

The fight is fixed. That means that you will have victory and your enemy is already defeated. It might not be a knockout in the beginning of round one. You might have to go the entire fight. But if you don't give up, you will win. Yes there is an enemy out there that seeks to destroy. You can never forget that the enemy wants to knock you out, but all you have to do is show up at the fight. Understand that the fight is on and that the fight is a fight for our lives. So today, I declare that the fight is on.

CHAPTER FOUR

The fight is on

For we wrestle not against flesh and blood, but against principalities, against powers, against the rulers of the darkness of this world, against spiritual wickedness in high places ~ Ephesians 6:12

The enemy fights with deceit and lies; the enemy fights without any mercy. He desires to assassinate you and he will stop at nothing to complete his task. The devil doesn't care what title or position you hold. As a matter of fact, the greater your anointing, the greater the fight. We all have visions, dreams, and aspirations, but the enemy tries to cloud your vision. You better know who your enemy is. If you don't, he will be sitting right in your waiting room, keeping you from ever entering the delivery room.

The fight is on and the battle starts in your mind. How is your mindset? Because the first place where we lose the battle is in our stinking thinking. Don't allow your limited thinking to allow you to live a limited life. We all have dreams, visions, and goals in life, but there will be times when the enemy will overshadow the vision that God has given us. He would love to steal our dreams, but the enemy cannot steal our dreams. But if we give them to him, the devil has a strategic plan of attack that he has planned for us. It is his goal to destroy our body, mind, and soul. His main purpose is to keep you from having what God has said that you can have.

For you to be able to defeat your enemy, you must understand his weapons. The enemy's arsenal is discouragement, fear, doubt, past mistakes, and failures. He uses these things to immobilize us and stop us right in our tracks. He understands that if he can wound you early in the battle, then you have already lost the war.

For as he thinketh in his heart, so is he. Eat and drink, saith he to thee, but his heart is not with thee ~ Proverbs 23:7

This passage of Scripture means that as a person thinks in his heart, so he is. Which means that our attitude determines how far we will go in life, because your attitude determines your actions. How we look at ourselves will determine what actions we will take in life.

The greatest battles that you will ever fight occur in your mind. Every day, we are bombarded with negative thoughts, fears, and doubts. What we need to realize is that the devil doesn't have any real power, but he is a liar and he is the father of all lies. He uses his weapons of mass destruction – lies and deception – to make us doubt the Word that God has spoken over our life.

It is important that we study the war tactics of Satan because he spends our lifetime studying us. That is why he attacks us when we are in our waiting room experience, when we are weak and vulnerable. He will make you feel like you are ugly, worthless, and useless. When you start to believe the lies of the enemy, then you will fall into a spirit of depression, low self-esteem, lack of self-confidence, anxiety, bitterness, and unforgiveness – these things will become strongholds in your life. A stronghold is a way of thinking that is deceptive. These strongholds affect the way that we think and the way that we act. Whatever we think about all the time is what we will become.

Circumstances and situations will greatly affect the way that we think about life. The enemy knows that our mind is very powerful and when he wants to defeat a child of God, he attacks their mind. If Satan can win the battle in your mind, then you are a fallen soldier.

One of Satan's strongest weapons is depression. Some signs of depression are sadness, discouragement, despair, and feelings of despondency. Long term depression can lead to suicidal thoughts or the actual act of committing suicide.

I recall a time in my life when I was in my waiting room experience, when I was waiting for God to deliver me from the grief that I was going through after the death of my son. Two months after he died, on his first birthday in heaven, I was so overcome with grief and sadness that I was contemplating committing suicide. I was staying at my sister's house because I was too scared to live alone. I was suffering anxiety and panic attacks on a regular basis, but I suffered in secret. That particular day, I was home alone and I remember going into the kitchen and pouring the entire bottle of blood pressure pills into my hand. I was trembling and crying uncontrollably. I just did not want to live without my son, but as I was about to take the pills, I heard a voice as clear as day saying, "If you take those pills, you will never see your son again because in hell will you open your eyes." I put the pills back into the bottle, mad at myself because now I was a real mess. I was too scared to die, and too scared to live. In my mind, I had nothing to live for and it was a hopeless situation. I was never going to come out of the waiting room. People all around me were getting called, but I was going to die in the waiting room. I wasn't even going to get a chance to see the doctor.

What a shame to make it to the hospital, but die in the waiting room. Hold on, my beloved. Don't die in the waiting room. Your appointment with destiny is coming soon!

Another weapon that Satan uses is discouragement. Discouragement is a part of life. Many times in our lives, we will face discouragement. We will feel discouraged when our finances are not right, or if we are having family problems, or when people disappoint us, or even when we disappoint people. Self-pity is our worst enemy and if we yield to it, we will be in a constant state of discouragement. The enemy loves to use the tool of discouragement to defeat us in battle. We will often find ourselves in a state of discouragement when we allow circumstances and situations to overwhelm us. Discouragement arrives when we are frustrated and often the enemy will frustrate our purpose as we allow the pressure, cares, and burdens of this world to prevent us from living the life that God has purposed for us.

I do not want to minimize the effects that discouragement has on our lives. Discouragement is a killer; it has killed many people's dreams, visions, and aspirations. Many of us face discouragement because we simply never had anyone to believe in us. Many people might have gone further than they did if they just had one person that saw the potential in them and told them they were worth it. It is funny how we can see the potential in other people, but we cannot see the treasure within ourselves. I used to be everyone's cheerleader. I would be on the sidelines yelling, "You can do it; if you can't do it, nobody can." But when it came to my own life, I was my own Debbie Downer.

Failure can lead to discouragement and the enemy will constantly throw our past failures and mistakes in our face. Discouragement makes us feel hopeless and in despair. You feel like the storms of life will never end. As soon as you come out of one storm, there is another storm on the horizon.

How can you overcome discouragement? You need to reflect on your past successes and failures and examine them to see if there are any patterns. What worked and what did not work? You can't do the same things the same old way and expect things to turn out differently.

You can beat discouragement by writing down your visions. You also need to take care of your body; your physical health is important. When you are tired and fatigued, that is when the enemy will strike. I have been overweight all my life and whenever I was going through a crisis, I ate. When I wanted to reward myself, my life was surrounded by food. When I was going through my waiting room experience, the enemy spoke to me and told me that I was the cause of my son's death because he was overweight. I spent months feeling guilty. The devil would tell me that I was fat and ugly and that I deserved everything that had happened to me. For months, I went through a serious battle with the enemy.

The people you surround yourself with are important because if you hang out with negative people, then you will always be downtrodden and discouraged. If they see that you are in a ditch, instead of pulling you out, they are pushing you further down. The old cliché that 'misery loves company' is true. The Word of God tells us if we resist the devil, he will flee from us, but most of the time we are shaking in our boots, so we find it hard to resist him.

Another weapon in Satan's arsenal is fear. Fear is a normal part of life. Everyone is afraid of something, whether they will admit it or not. People are afraid of the dark, bugs, planes, boats, heights – just to name a few. I have a few fears myself: I am afraid of flying, heights, and dogs. Some of these fears have a real effect on my quality of life. Because I am afraid of flying, whenever I travel I must go by car, train, or bus which takes longer to get there, therefore limiting the places I can go.

Today, people are far more afraid than they were before 911. When we turn on the television, all that we hear is bad news. The media spreads fear and propaganda. We are afraid of terrorists and thieves and robbers, afraid of large crowds – sometimes we are so fearful that we do not want to go about our daily activities. We have a fear of change, a fear of failure. Fear will stagnate you and rob you of your ability to even try. Fear plays into the hands of the enemy. Fear will make the strongest person weak. It is fear that whispers in your ear that you are sick and you will never get well. How many times do you think that the woman with the issue of blood was afraid that she would never get well? The Bible doesn't say, but I can imagine every time she went to a new doctor and they could not stop the bleeding, she got just a little more fearful.

The enemy has a plan. He knows that if he can keep you afraid of your own shadow, then he has rendered you helpless. Fear stops us from stepping into our destiny. Instead of moving forward, we are standing still or moving backward. Fear is natural and it will keep us safe in harmful situations. If you are home alone and you hear a noise downstairs, fear will make you proceed with caution. If you are walking down the street and you see a pit-bull, or even if you are getting in your car in a dark area, fear is helpful. But when fear takes over your life and leads you to anxiety and panic attacks, in this case, fear has become a stronghold in your life. Fear is not tangible or visible, but exists in our mind.

Another weapon that the enemy has is doubt. The enemy will cause you to doubt yourself. If you don't believe in yourself, you will not get far in life. If you do not deem that you can, then you probably will not. Often in life, instead of upgrading ourselves, we will downgrade ourselves. We are constantly doubting that we are good enough to live our dream life, to walk into our purpose. We doubt our gifts and talents.

> *"Don't let others tell you what you can't do. Don't let the limitations of others limit your vision. If you can remove your self-doubt and believe in yourself, you can achieve what you never thought possible." ~ Ray T Bennett*

Many people learn to believe at an early age that we are lacking in some aspect of our lives and we are not good enough. We feel that we are not smart enough or thin enough. Doubt is basically a deficit of confidence in your gifts and talents. If you experience doubt in your life, you will not even try because you have a fear of failure, and this will lead to a feeling of frustration. If you are constantly doubting the choices that you make, you question whether or not you can make the right decisions.

One of the most lethal weapons that the enemy uses is our past. We are so busy looking back at our past that we cannot look forward to our future. Every one of us has something in our past that causes us shame, something that we would not want anyone to ever find out. We have so many skeletons in our closet and those are the things that the enemy will use to keep us in mental bondage. We regret a lot of decisions that we made in our past. We often look back and wish that we could have a do-over. Many times, we hold resentful and unforgiving feelings in our hearts against people that did us wrong or hurt us. Some of us have had a painful past, some of us have been physically or emotionally abused, and we cannot let it go. Some people have suffered losses that they can't seem to bounce back from.

The failures of our past can be an obstacle to us reaching our destiny. Many people are living in bondage to their past mistakes and every time we think that we are over it, there is somebody to remind us of who we used to be. The chains are so tight that we are unable to take the steps to try again. Many people allow our past mistakes and failures to control our futures. Some of you have sabotaged every good thing that came into your life because you were so busy looking at everything through the dirty lens of your past, you could not see past your prior disappointments, hurts, and past wounds.

"We are products of our past, but we do not have to be prisoners of it." ~ Rick Warren.

We allow the pain of our past to rule us in our present and to predetermine our future. It is hard to drive forward on life's windy roads while you continue to look out your rearview mirror. Looking back at your past will cause you regret. Regret is unhealthy when it leads us to having feelings of hopelessness. We tell ourselves things like: "What difference does it make? My life is already messed up. I only deserve the crumbs off the table. I can never have anything more than second best. There is no need for me to even try for better."

It would be awesome if we never faced any problems in our past. But that is impossible. Many of us carry excessive baggage from our past. We carry depression, guilt, and fear. Every day, people carry scars from their past, and often these scars are still painful and continue to hold us down.

CHAPTER FIVE

The fight continues

Quenched the violence of the fire, escaped the edge of the sword, out of weakness were made strong, waxed valiant in fight, turned to fight the armies of aliens. ~ Hebrews 11:34

There is a constant battle going on for the control of our minds. The fight is between Satan, the father of lies, and us. What are we battling against? We fight against lust, bitterness, drugs, alcohol, work, unforgiveness, attitude and our past. There are times when you will feel that you are in so deep over your head that you will never have victory over your life. Satan wants to keep us in bondage thinking about the cares of this world:

Whose end is destruction, whose God is their belly, and whose glory is in their shame, who mind earthly things. ~ Philippians 3:19

If our mind is controlled by earthly things and if we quickly give in to those things that make the flesh feel good to us, then we have already thrown in the towel and cried 'uncle.' We must first realize that we are overcomers and that we are able to win the battle that is in our minds.

By this point in the book, I pray that you have declared war on the devil and decided to be a victor rather than a victim. The fight is on. Before you enter warfare, you must understand that the fight will not be easy. The devil will appear at times to have an unfair advantage. The devil is fighting for keeps, but what you are fighting for is so much more important – you are fighting for your life back.

You must remember that even in your waiting period, God has your back. He is your defender. You do not have to fight by yourself.

Ye shall not have to fight in this battle: set yourselves, stand ye still, and see the salvation of the Lord with you, O Judah and Jerusalem: fear not, nor be dismayed; tomorrow go against them, for the Lord will be with you. ~ 2 Chronicles 20:17

In this life, we will face many obstacles. We will run smack into detours, setbacks, and disappointments. If there is a devil, there will be a battle, but in this passage of Scripture, God is reminding King Jehoshaphat that the battle is not his. The first thing that the king did before the battle was to declare a fast and then he sought the Lord in prayer. The king knew that he needed God because there was no humanly way that they would be able to defeat their enemies. The king knew that God was all he had, but how many people know that God is all we need when we go into battle?

The Word of God assures us that in the end we will be victorious. Satan knows that when you invite Jesus into the fight, when you hold up the rope and allow Jesus into the ring, then the fight for you is over. That's why the enemy wants to destroy you before this happens. That's why he plans a sneak attack and he hits you hard enough to knock you down. He wants to kill us before we realize that the fight is fixed and we already have victory. It is God's plan for us to be victorious.

Nay, in all these things we are more than conquerors through Him that loved us. ~ Romans 8:37

The devil will stop at nothing to bring you down. When the enemy thinks that he has you cornered, he will come out swinging your past in front of you. Let me tell you a little secret: all men will fall at sometime in their life, but only the great one gets back up again. If you do not bury your past, then it will bury you in guilt and shame. We do not have to be chained to our hurtful past. We do not have to nurse the same wounds night after night. We do not have to cry over our yesterdays. God has something greater for you. The harder the battle, the greater the victory. God will never give up on you because He has too much of an investment in your life.

During your years of battle, you might have been used, misused, and abused. There are those who you thought you could trust, but during your greatest battle they turned their back on you. I was let down by people who, in my wildest dreams, I never thought they would drop me. It hurt like hell when I realized that not everyone wanted me to get out of the waiting room. Some people just came to see me in the waiting room because they only wanted to show up to see if I was still hurting, if I was still broken. They were not going to celebrate me, but they were only tolerating me and I had to realize that everybody could not go with me to another level. I had to learn to let go of relationships.

When it is time to let go, when people want to walk out of your life, let them. Stop holding people prisoner in your life. Give them parole; let them walk. Because God has those people who are waiting for you to reach your destiny. I had to understand that God also removes people from our lives because some people are meant to be in your life for a reason and a season, and when that season is over they have to go because they have already served their purpose.

God has more for you this day than what you lived through yesterday. Don't give up the fight; the earthly things that you fought hard to hold on to are not even worth holding on to. The enemy wants to make your future look as bleak as your past. He wants to knock the fight out of you.

Be sober, be vigilant; because your adversary the devil, as a roaring lion, walketh about, seeking whom he may devour ~ 1 Peter 5:8

The devil doesn't just want to stop you – he wants to destroy you. He wants to make us ineffective in the kingdom of God. He doesn't want us to live up to our Godly potential. The Word says that the enemy has a plan, a scheme to attack us. The enemy doesn't just show up to the battle, but he comes strategically and what he wants is our minds. Do not take Satan lightly because he is a seasoned veteran; he has fought many a war and left many casualties. Satan desires to control your mind because he knows that you can win the battle and eventually the war.

There is greatness in each one of us. When you are in the waiting room, it is hard to remember the promises that God has spoken over your life. I do not have itching ears, but I believe the words that are spoken over my life are in agreement with what God has already shown me. The truth be told, I could not see them coming to fruition while I was in my waiting room experience. If God promises you something, it will come to manifestation, but that reality doesn't stop Satan from trying to postpone the fulfillment of God's promise in your life. Satan cannot stop what God has ordained, but he can cause you to doubt it, which causes a delay.

What God has said must come to pass. It might not come in the package that you thought it would, delivered by the person or situation that you thought would deliver it. It might not come when you want it to because God's timing is not our timing. I want to encourage someone who might still be sitting in God's waiting room, wondering if you are ever going to come out and if your life is over – yes, yes you will come out. And when you make it out, you will be more anointed than you were when you went in. If God said it, then it must come to fruition.

While you are in your waiting room, Satan will try to kill God's will for your life, but it won't work.

Being confident of this very thing, that he which hath begun a good work in you will perform it until the day of Jesus Christ ~ Philippians 1:6

Despite what it looks like, you are not a finished product. Your chapter is not over. If God said it, I believe it and that settles it. God will bring to pass what He has said in your life. You do not have enough enemies and hell has no power to stop what God has already predestined. The road to your destiny is full of disappointments, valleys, endings and beginnings, setbacks and detours. No matter what you are going through you have the promise that all things work out…

…for the good to them that love God, to them who are called according to his purpose ~ Romans 8:28

It is time for you to expect to win. When we lose our air of expectancy, then the enemy will trick you into believing that you cannot win. It is time for you to get up out of your comfort zone, stop the pity party, and come out with your dukes raised and fighting. My pastor Bishop William Billups often says that it is not the size of the dog, but the size of the fight that is in the dog.

For you to fight to win, you must be tired – you must be sick and tired of coming to the battle day after day, but not fighting. You must be tired of being used and abused. You must be tired of being broke, tired of living in yesterday and allowing yesterday to abort your future. You must come to the point that you are weary of being lonely and defective.

I am praying that someone right now is tired of moaning and groaning, tired of getting life's leftovers. You are drained from being knocked down by the devil; you are depleted by living beneath your past instead of living victoriously in the present. It is time to soar above your situations and circumstances. It is just when Satan has you on the ropes that you must come out fighting. He will not stop at any tricks or deception, so you must be willing and ready to fight.

You can decide today that you want control over your life and your mind. You must remember that the enemy is not fighting you for where you are now, he is fighting you to stop you from what you are to become. Satan is afraid of your future – that's why he wants to keep you chained to your past. People who are not going through anything are those people who are not going anywhere.

You must remember that Satan is powerless. We allow him to make giants in our lives. For these giants to control us, we must relinquish the power to them. You can decide today that you want authority over your destiny. Decree and declare that you are tired of living with a war-torn mind. It is time to put your war clothes on and choose your weapon because the fight is on.

Wait! I hear someone calling your name. Your wait is over and it is time for you to go into the delivery room because giants do die. Like the songwriter says: the bigger they are, the harder they fall.

CHAPTER SIX

Giants do die

And there went out a champion out of the camp of the Philistines, named Goliath of Gath, whose height was six cubits and a span. ~ 1 Samuel 17:4

At some point in our lives, we are going to face some giants. It does not matter what your socioeconomic status is, whether you are rich or poor. It doesn't matter what political party you belong to, republican or democrat. It doesn't matter what your gender is, male or female. And it doesn't matter what religious organization you belong to, if you are Pentecostal, Baptist or Methodist. During certain seasons in your life, you will face some giants.

Giants will appear in different chapters in your life, from the waiting room, to the delivery room, to the recovery room. There are giants of discouragement, doubts, low self-esteem, or your past. A giant is an unresolved problem that grew into a stronghold and eventually grew into a full-grown giant. We spend a lifetime trying to avoid our giants, pretending they don't exist, or simply running from them. It does not matter how long these giants have existed in your life. I want to encourage you that in the delivery room, giants do die.

There's a song that says: the bigger they are, the harder they fall. But I must inform you of something – giants don't just fall dead. You must be courageous enough to be a demon-chaser, giant-slayer. You were anointed for the battle in the waiting room, but it was not time yet.

I had fainted, unless I had believed to see the goodness of the Lord in the land of the living. Wait on the Lord: be of good courage, and he shall strengthen thine heart: wait, I say, on the Lord. ~ Psalm 27:13-14

Don't give up. It's time for you to be delivered. It will not be easy, but you are prepared this time for the battle. At this point, you know who you are and what your personal issues are. You recognize the enemy and his strategic plan for battle, and you have decided that it is time to fight. The stakes are high, but you want to take back everything that the enemy stole from you. The only things standing in your way are your giants. It doesn't matter how big your giants appear, they can come down. One of the most famous giants in the Bible is Goliath:

> [1] *Now the Philistines gathered together their armies to battle, and were gathered together at Shochoh, which belongeth to Judah, and pitched between Shochoh and Azekah, in Ephesdammim.*
> [2] *And Saul and the men of Israel were gathered together, and pitched by the valley of Elah, and set the battle in array against the Philistines.*

3 *And the Philistines stood on a mountain on the*
one side, and Israel stood on a mountain on the
other side: and there was a valley between them.
4 *And there went out a champion out of the camp*
of the Philistines, named Goliath, of Gath, whose
height was six cubits and a span.
5 *And he had an helmet of brass upon his head,*
and he was armed with a coat of mail; and the
weight of the coat was five thousand shekels of
brass.
6 *And he had greaves of brass upon his legs, and a*
target of brass between his shoulders.
7 *And the staff of his spear was like a weaver's*
beam; and his spear's head weighed six hundred
shekels of iron: and one bearing a shield went
before him.
8 *And he stood and cried unto the armies of Israel,*
and said unto them, Why are ye come out to set
your battle in array? am not I a Philistine, and ye

servants to Saul? choose you a man for you, and let him come down to me.

9 *If he be able to fight with me, and to kill me, then will we be your servants: but if I prevail against him, and kill him, then shall ye be our servants, and serve us.*

10 *And the Philistine said, I defy the armies of Israel this day; give me a man, that we may fight together.*

11 *When Saul and all Israel heard those words of the Philistine, they were dismayed, and greatly afraid. (1 Samuel 17:1-11)*

For forty days, the giant Goliath had bullied the children of Israel. He had them terrified and scared. Not one man was willing to fight him. What has been terrifying you? What is bullying you? Is it depression, fear, low self-esteem, your past mistakes and failures, some deep secret that you are ashamed of? What giant is keeping you cowering in the corner scared to come out?

David's father sends him to check on his brothers and to bring them food and supplies. When he arrives on the scene, he sees the big bad bully taunting the children of Israel.

12Now David was the son of that Ephrathite of Bethlehemjudah, whose name was Jesse; and he had eight sons: and the man went among men for an old man in the days of Saul.

13 And the three eldest sons of Jesse went and followed Saul to the battle: and the names of his three sons that went to the battle were Eliab the firstborn, and next unto him Abinadab, and the third Shammah.

14 And David was the youngest: and the three eldest followed Saul.

15 But David went and returned from Saul to feed his father's sheep at Bethlehem.

16 And the Philistine drew near morning and evening, and presented himself forty days.

17 *And Jesse said unto David his son, Take now
for thy brethren an ephah of this parched corn,
and these ten loaves, and run to the camp to thy
brethren;*
18 *And carry these ten cheeses unto the captain of
their thousand, and look how thy brethren fare,
and take their pledge.*
19 *Now Saul, and they, and all the men of Israel,
were in the valley of Elah, fighting with the
Philistines.*
20 *And David rose up early in the morning, and
left the sheep with a keeper, and took, and went,
as Jesse had commanded him; and he came to the
trench, as the host was going forth to the fight,
and shouted for the battle.*
21 *For Israel and the Philistines had put the battle
in array, army against army.*
22 *And David left his carriage in the hand of the
keeper of the carriage, and ran into the army, and
came and saluted his brethren.*

23 *And as he talked with them, behold, there came
up the champion, the Philistine of Gath, Goliath
by name, out of the armies of the Philistines, and
spake according to the same words: and David
heard them.*
24 *And all the men of Israel, when they saw the
man, fled from him, and were sore afraid.*
25 *And the men of Israel said, Have ye seen this
man that is come up? surely to defy Israel is he
come up: and it shall be, that the man who killeth
him, the king will enrich him with great riches,
and will give him his daughter, and make his
father's house free in Israel.*
26 *And David spake to the men that stood by him,
saying, What shall be done to the man that killeth
this Philistine, and taketh away the reproach from
Israel? for who is this uncircumcised Philistine,
that he should defy the armies of the living God?*

[27] *And the people answered him after this manner, saying, So shall it be done to the man that killeth him.*

[28] *And Eliab his eldest brother heard when he spake unto the men; and Eliab's anger was kindled against David, and he said, Why camest thou down hither? and with whom hast thou left those few sheep in the wilderness? I know thy pride, and the naughtiness of thine heart; for thou art come down that thou mightest see the battle.*

[29] *And David said, What have I now done? Is there not a cause?* (1 *Samuel 17:12-29)*

To understand David's battle with the giant, we must take a glimpse into David's past. For some of you to slay your giants, you are going to have to look back into your past and see where you are stagnated. What in your past has caused you so much pain that you cannot seem to let it go? In the 16th verse of 1 Samuel, David was anointed to be the next King of

Israel. He was ordained, anointed, and appointed, but he still was not ready to step into that position.

Many of us have been anointed, but it is just not your time yet. God will place you into His waiting room and He will use these times of waiting to prepare you for your next level in Him. He will test and try you to see if you will be able to stand when troubles come. We simply must wait on God's timing.

David waited on the Lord. He was appointed to be king at sixteen, but did not become king until he was thirty. David went through a lot of disappointments, heartaches, and failure while he waited. After being anointed King, he went back to the field tending his father's sheep. How many of you know that God has anointed you for greatness, but you are still in the field? Don't be bitter, get better while you wait. David was in the field until his father called him into his destiny. David's father called him out of the field and asked him to go into the valley where his brothers were in a battle with the Philistine. Jesse wanted

David to check on his brother and bring them food and supplies.

God will always place you in the right place at the right time when He is ready to use you, when He is ready to call you out of the waiting room. Listen closely! Somebody is being called out of the waiting room. Is it you?

As David was delivering the food, he heard Goliath issuing his daily challenge and David wanted to know what the man would receive that could defeat Goliath. Meanwhile, while he was talking to the man, his brother overheard the conversation and got angry with David. Maybe his older brother was jealous of the position that David already had, or maybe he was ashamed because he was afraid of the giant, like all of the other soldiers were greatly afraid.

There are seasons in our lives where we are fighting in battles that seem impossible to win. It appears that the odds have been stacked against us in the battle and the enemy appears to have the upper hand. It is so overwhelming that we become frustrated, because the challenge is so demanding that we are afraid to fight. The fear stagnates us and the battles become so large that they appear larger than life.

The story, even though it was familiar, did not carry any real significance until I began to face certain situations in my life. And it was during these times that I thought I was in a battle against something that I could not win. It was then that the story of David and Goliath had practical application to my life. I remember sitting in Sunday school and painting a mental picture of the Philistine champion. He was over nine feet tall and the armor that he wore weighed over 150 pounds.

What does your giant look like? What is the visual picture that you have in your mind of your bigger-than-life giant? What is a giant? A giant is anything that stands between you and your dreams. Some of us are facing similar battles in our life; it is winner take all. If you lose this battle, you will once again be enslaved to the devil. The children of Israel believed that they were in a no-win situation. Because of the size of the giant, they were already defeated mentally. The adage is true: if you do not believe that you can, then you won't be able to.

The battle begins in our mind and it can either end in victory or defeat. As we read in the last chapter, fear is one of the most potent weapons of the enemy. There are many kinds of fear. There is claustrophobia, which is the fear of small enclosed places such as an elevator. I suffered from acrophobia, which is the fear of heights. I am believing God that He will deliver me from that fear.

The nation of Israel was so fearful that this fear stopped them from even envisioning victory. The same way that fear can stop us from experiencing spiritual victory. Goliath was the children of Israel's giant to overcome and it did not make it any easier that their leader was just as scared as they were. Saul, the children of Israel's leader, was already in a defeated state of mind. He was going through some personal issues of his own. Saul was chosen, anointed, and appointed by God, but he was disobedient and thus the spirit of the Lord was no longer dwelling within him. It is impossible to lead God's people when God no longer has your back.

As I think about the Israelite soldiers, I think about the bully in the lunchroom. Every day, they take your lunch money and taunt you, and you are so afraid of them that, day after day, you continue to hand over your lunch money. This daily encounter makes you feel weak and helpless. Every morning and every night for forty days and forty nights, the children of Israel were terrified and filled with fear. For forty days, Saul and his army would wake up to Goliath's challenge, therefore day after day, they had a fearful standoff with the giant.

How many days and nights do we wake up to our same giants and we stand trembling, too scared to fight? How many times do we waste our time facing that same giant ineffectively? How many times do we get back in bed, cover our head, and just wish our giant will go away? Or even worse, we can do like the children of Israel and run away from our giants.

David faced a physical giant in his life, but we face many different giants. Some of the giants that we face are relationship giants– problems with our family, spouses, or children. We have emotional problems – worries, fears, doubts, grief, and depression, just to name a few. There are also financial giants – loss of a job or being underpaid. We have giants of rejection, failure, and our past. These giants will often taunt us saying, "I told you that you were not good enough. You are not smart enough. You will never be able to hold your head above water; you will never rise above poverty level. You will never be able to save your marriage; he never wanted you in the first place. You will never get over your past mistakes and failures." These giants will stand and say, "You will never get past me." These giants will try to stop us from achieving our God-given dreams.

While you are in this situation, your situation looks bleak and hopeless. While you are in the valley you do not see any possible way out. What are your personal giants? What is that thing that you cannot seem to overcome? What are the obstacles and hurdles that you need to get over? These giants may be physical, mental, emotional, or even spiritual. We often ask ourselves if giants do die, and if they do die, how can we kill them? We know that David did kill his physical giant. What can we learn from David's military strategy that can help us to defeat our personal giants?

> 31 *And when the words were heard which David spake, they rehearsed them before Saul: and he sent for him.*

[32] *And David said to Saul, Let no man's heart fail
because of him; thy servant will go and fight with
this Philistine.*
[33] *And Saul said to David, Thou art not able to go
against this Philistine to fight with him: for thou
art but a youth, and he a man of war from his
youth.*
[34] *And David said unto Saul, Thy servant kept his
father's sheep, and there came a lion, and a bear,
and took a lamb out of the flock:*
[35] *And I went out after him, and smote him, and
delivered it out of his mouth: and when he arose
against me, I caught him by his beard, and smote
him, and slew him.*
[36] *Thy servant slew both the lion and the bear: and
this uncircumcised Philistine shall be as one of
them, seeing he hath defied the armies of the
living God.*
[37] *David said moreover, The Lord that delivered
me out of the paw of the lion, and out of the paw*

of the bear, he will deliver me out of the hand of
this Philistine. And Saul said unto David, Go, and
the Lord be with thee.
38 *And Saul armed David with his armor, and he*
put an helmet of brass upon his head; also he
armed him with a coat of mail.
39 *And David girded his sword upon his armor,*
and he assayed to go; for he had not proved it.
And David said unto Saul, I cannot go with these;
for I have not proved them. And David put them
off him.
40 *And he took his staff in his hand, and chose him*
five smooth stones out of the brook, and put them
in a shepherd's bag which he had, even in a scrip;
and his sling was in his hand: and he drew near to
the Philistine.
41 *And the Philistine came on and drew near unto*
David; and the man that bare the shield went
before him.

42 *And when the Philistine looked about, and saw
David, he disdained him: for he was but a youth,
and ruddy, and of a fair countenance.*
43 *And the Philistine said unto David, Am I a dog,
that thou comest to me with staves? And the
Philistine cursed David by his gods.*
44 *And the Philistine said to David, Come to me,
and I will give thy flesh unto the fowls of the air,
and to the beasts of the field.*
45 *Then said David to the Philistine, Thou comest
to me with a sword, and with a spear, and with a
shield: but I come to thee in the name of the Lord
of hosts, the God of the armies of Israel, whom
thou hast defied.*
46 *This day will the Lord deliver thee into mine
hand; and I will smite thee, and take thine head
from thee; and I will give the carcasses of the host
of the Philistines this day unto the fowls of the air,
and to the wild beasts of the earth; that all the
earth may know that there is a God in Israel.*

47 *And all this assembly shall know that the Lord*
saveth not with sword and spear: for the battle is
the Lord's, and he will give you into our hands.
48 *And it came to pass, when the Philistine arose,*
and came and drew nigh to meet David, that
David hasted, and ran toward the army to meet
the Philistine.
49 *And David put his hand in his bag, and took*
thence a stone, and slang it, and smote the
Philistine in his forehead, that the stone sunk into
his forehead; and he fell upon his face to the
earth.
50 *So David prevailed over the Philistine with a*
sling with a stone, and smote the Philistine, and
slew him; but there was no and sword in the hand
of David.
51 *Therefore David ran, and stood upon the*
Philistine, and took his sword, and drew it out of
the sheath thereof, and slew him, and cut off his

head therewith. And when the Philistines saw
their champion was dead, they fled.
52 *And the men of Israel and of Judah arose, and*
shouted, and pursued the Philistines, until thou
come to the valley, and to the gates of Ekron. And
the wounded of the Philistines fell down by the
way to Shaaraim, even unto Gath, and unto
Ekron.
53 *And the children of Israel returned from*
chasing after the Philistines, and they spoiled
their tents.
54 *And David took the head of the Philistine, and*
brought it to Jerusalem; but he put his armor in
his tent.
55 *And when Saul saw David go forth against the*
Philistine, he said unto Abner, the captain of the
host, Abner, whose son is this youth? And Abner
said, As thy soul liveth, O king, I cannot tell.
56 *And the king said, Enquire thou whose son the*
stripling is.

[57] *And as David returned from the slaughter of the Philistine, Abner took him, and brought him before Saul with the head of the Philistine in his hand.*

[58] *And Saul said to him, Whose son art thou, thou young man? And David answered, I am the son of thy servant Jesse the Bethlehemite. (1 Samuel 17:31-58)*

When David tells Saul that he is willing and ready to fight the giant, Saul takes one look at David and says, "You are not prepared to fight this mammoth, violent man. You are just a young boy and Goliath has been terrorizing people from basically birth." David was destined to be King, but there was one thing standing between him and his kingdom. David had been in the waiting room for seventeen long years, but now it was his time. When it is your time to be delivered, can't no devil or giant from hell stop you.

Let's take another look at David's giant. He was standing nine feet tall, he was enormous, and he was a bully. He used the tactic of intimidation to keep his enemies stagnated and stuck in fear. He used his massive size and killer reputation to keep the Israelite army at bay and cowering in the corner, scared of their own shadows. Every day, he came out wearing his full armor, dressed for battle and calling out the children of Israel. I can hear him saying, "Come out, come out from wherever you are, scaredy cats." Goliath was cocky and full of himself. He would march up and down teasing and taunting. Goliath was a fighter from youth and he just knew that he could not be beaten. So he challenged them to send one of their best men out to take him on, to fight him one on one. They did not need their armies; this was going to be hand-to-hand combat and the winner would take all. Goliath was the biggest, baddest soldier around. I imagine that after every encounter with the children of Israel, he would go back to camp and declare, "Not today, they all punked out again today. But I will go back before the sun goes down and see if there is one that is bad enough to step to me."

This happened for forty straight days and nights. Goliath would go to the hill and challenge someone to come and fight him. One man stopped an entire army in their tracks, one giant stood between them and victory, and what made the situation worse was that even the leader of the army was scared senseless. 1 Samuel 17, verse 11 says Saul and all Israel were dismayed and terrified.

How does it look that you are supposed to be leading the people in battle and you're scared? As a leader, you are supposed to be the first partaker. Saul should have been the first one to offer to fight the giant. How can you expect your followers to do something that you are not capable of doing? At this point in Saul's life, he was facing many personal battles. He was disobedient and the spirit of the Lord had left him. He was left to handle life using his own strength. Sal was the first king of Israel and he had disobeyed God early in his career. When God told him to destroy the Amalekites and all of their stuff, Saul decided to do otherwise; therefore his life was in a downward spiral. He wasn't fit to be king and that's why David had already been appointed that position by God. Saul was depressed and oppressed and lacked self-confidence, thus he was already defeated in his mind.

When you lose God's favor in your life, that is a lonely place to be in – surrounded by people, but being tormented by thoughts from your past. And along comes David, the little shepherd. You can still smell the stench of the sheep dung emanating from his skin. As David is looking for his older brothers, he sees the big giant towering over the children of Israel making his daily challenge:

> *This day I defy the ranks of Israel! Give me a man and let us fight each other. ~ 1 Samuel 17:10 (NIV)*

David's focus is no longer on finding his brother. Now his focus is on the giant. David could not comprehend why no one was willing to fight this man. When David offered to fight the giant, the first hater was not a stranger, but his own brother.

Sometimes our greatest battle is with those we call friend, or even worse, family. David's brother tried to impress him. He asked him, "What are you doing here? And while you are here being nosy, who is watching your sheep, little shepherd boy?"

His brother's obvious jealousy did not stop him. David could have gone back to the field with his head stuck between his tail, but no. He went to Saul and said, "Let me go fight this uncircumcised Philistine."

And even though no one else was willing to go, Saul still questioned if David was ready for the challenge. He said, "You are just a little boy and this man is a killer.

David said, "While I was in the field watching my father's sheep and when the lion and the bear came, I killed them and rescued the sheep out of the mouth of the lion and the bear. My God was with me during those times and the Lord is going to be with me when I kill the giant." Saul tried to dress David up in his clothes with his weapons, but David said, "I cannot wear your clothes I have not proven them, so I have to go with what I know."

When we are facing our giants, what worked for the next person might not work for you. The Bible tells us that David goes to fight the giant and when he comes face to face with the giant, Goliath laughs in David's face and declares, "This must be a joke. This is who they sent to fight me? A little shepherd boy? What, am I a dog? They must have forgotten who I am and just how big and bad I am. This must be a joke."

David told Goliath, "*You come to me with a sword, with a spear. And with a javelin. But I come to you in the name of the Lord of hosts, the God of the armies of Israel." (1 Samuel 17:45)*

David ran toward the giant and said, "Today is the day that you are going down." You see, David had never fought a giant, but he knew that the same God that was there when he fought the lion and the bear would help him fight this Philistine. The Bible says that David picks up five stones. The first one brought down the giant and he used the giant's own sword to cut off the giant's head and brought it to Saul. David picked up five stones because he knew that when he brought down Goliath, that was going to make him a wanted man.

So, you might be saying that David's giant was a physical one, but how am I going to defeat my devil, and not only defeat it, but kill it at its root? The first thing that you need to do is to get delivered from people and the criticism of people. David did not listen to his brother when they called him a little dirty shepherd boy and questioned his integrity and the motives that were in his heart. He did not listen to Saul, the leader of the army who told him that he was too young and inexperienced to fight the devil. What giants are you facing in your life today? Is it fear, depression, heartache? What do you call your giant? How long has your giant been taunting you? How long has your giant had your paralyzed with fear?

There are people in your life that, like Saul, will tell you that you cannot do it. Some of these people are intentional dream killers; they want to kill your dreams. And then there are unintentional dream killers, those like Saul that mean well, but they cannot see what God has placed inside of you. They cannot see the greatness that is in your life. You cannot expect someone who has rocked their dreams to sleep to get excited about yours. You cannot ask financial advice from someone who is broke.

There are two types of dream killers: one is those old jealous folks who are strategically placed in your life to kill your dreams, and then there are other people who simply tell you all of the negative things that you might encounter as you chase after your dreams. For example, if you tell your friend you want to write a book, she might tell you that it is hard to get a book published traditionally. Or if you want to go back to school, they might say you are too old to go back to school. What are you going to do with a degree? Now these people mean well, but they are looking with their natural eye. They can't see what God sees in you. They cannot see the greatness that is deposited in you. You are great and God has a plan for your life.

I understand that your giant looks enormous and some of you have been running from this thing for a long time. Many a night you have cried yourself to sleep; the pain was just too great. There are things that you have been struggling with your whole life. This giant has been teasing you and calling you names. I want to encourage you that you can kill your giants and be set free. The devil cannot stop God's plan for your life. He can delay it, but only you can stop it.

God is about to help you slay some giants and those people who have been sitting by waiting for you to fail, pushing you into a pit, once you are delivered they are really going to be mad. Get ready for some upset folks in your life. They came to pull the plug, but God has you breathing on your own now. A lot of people know your story and some of them are still wondering how you made it. They are talking about you now, but when God gets through with you, everybody in town is going to be talking about you.

Yes, my dear, you are a giant-killer and after you are finished reading this book, the giants that have been standing in your way will no longer be there. There will be dead heads cut off this time. You know for sure they will not resurface tomorrow, next week, or next year. It will not be an easy fight, but nothing worth having comes easy. It's time to stop being a coward and running from your problems, and run straight for that giant. It is time to stop allowing that sickness to control your life and declare, "I will live my best life ever." Your struggles are over if you can just believe and know the power that you have inside of you. You, like David, are a giant-killer and you can be signed, sealed, and delivered, but you must soar above your circumstances.

CHAPTER SEVEN

Soar above your circumstances

But they that wait upon the Lord shall renew their strength; they shall mount up with wings as eagles; they shall run, and not be weary; and they shall walk, and not faint. ~ Isaiah 40:31

What's your purpose? Everyone is born with their own unique purpose in life, but not everyone will live a purpose-filled life. Many people's dreams and visions will succumb to the many obstacles and oppositions that they face in life. To be able to soar above your circumstances, you must decide what motivates you, what drives you, what is your why, and why you want to fulfill your dreams and visions. The secret to soaring above your circumstances is asking yourself, does your purpose in life tug at your heartstrings harder than your past mistakes and failures, your fear of failure, and your self-doubt? If your purpose in life is stronger than those obstacles, then you will be able to soar above your circumstances.

The adage that anything worth having is worth working for is true – and it is not going to be a flowery bed of ease. You will need determination and must make great sacrifices to pursue your purpose, dreams, and visions. To soar above your circumstances, it will not be enough just to have a dream or a vision. To live out your purpose, you must also have a plan of action. How are you going to live your purpose-driven life when it seems like the odds are stacked up against you? You must face these setbacks with the resolve that you will not allow anything or anybody to keep you from your purpose.

Some people can soar above their circumstances and attain their dreams and visions, and others do not.

Do you ever wonder why some people are successful and others are not? One of the reasons why some people never achieve their purpose in life is that they do not define their dreams and goals; they do not know what they want to do. Fear cripples many people's dreams. They have a fear of failure or a fear of succeeding. Many allow the lack of resources to stop them. Many are procrastinators and keep putting their dreams off year after year. Many suffer from self-doubt and low self-confidence. If you surround yourself with negative people, that can kill your dreams before you even conceive them.

If you are going to soar above your circumstances, you must believe that you are meant for greatness. You are bigger than your circumstances. Your life is not limited to your present bank account, educational level, current relationships, or past mistakes and failures. You must rise above the pain and disappointments. Whatever you are going through, you do not have to accept that as your norm. You were designed for a purpose. Do not allow anyone to count you out.

There is a story about a donkey that fell into a well. The donkey was old so they decided that he was not worth saving. They started to throw dirt on him, but he would shake it off of his back, packing the dirt under his feet as he stepped on it. When the well was filled with dirt, the donkey started to rise in spite of his circumstances, and when he reached the top he just stepped out. So, whatever situation or circumstances that you find yourself in, you can shake it off. Put it under your feet and rise above your circumstances.

When the storms of life come, we must be like the eagles. An eagle knows that a storm is coming. Before it comes, he will fly to a high spot and wait for the storm. When the storm comes, the eagle will spread its wings. The wind will take the eagle above the storm and the eagle rises above it. The eagle does not escape the storm, but soars above the storm instead. It uses the storm to lift it higher. No matter who you are, you are going to face some storms in your life. You will endure storms of sickness, loss of loved ones, disappointments, failure, and tragedy. But when the storms of life come, we can rise above them and soar like an eagle. You can soar above your circumstances.

You can walk through your fire. In September of 2016, the apartment building that I lived in went up in smoke. My apartment didn't burn, but I lost most of my possessions. It was during this time that I was writing Dream Killers and this book, and I felt like once again the devil had knocked me down. It was a physical fire that turned into a spiritual one. I was homeless and had to stay with my mother in a one bedroom apartment with my daughter. I am thanking God that I could stay at my mother's because I did not have renter's insurance, and when I went to Social Services they sent me to a bedbug-ridden, fleabag motel. I stayed there an hour and had to go back to my mother's. There were many people who were a blessing to me during this time, but once again, the people I thought were going to be there were nowhere to be found.

Fire has many attributes, but one of the main things about fire is that it hurts. There are many varieties of fire – there is financial fire, sickness fire, and physical and emotional fire. Some of you reading this book have been through some fiery trials and you did not think that you were going to make it out. I am encouraging you right now to walk through your fire. Don't get burned in the fire, just keep walking. Many of you are going through fire because you are going to a place in God where the devil can do you no harm. God has a higher level for you in Him. The fire was not meant to kill you.

> *Beloved, think it not strange concerning the fiery trial which is to try you, as though some strange thing happened unto you: But rejoice, inasmuch as ye are partakers of Christ's sufferings; that,*

when his glory shall be revealed, ye may be glad also with exceeding joy. ~ 1 Peter 4:12-13

Most people don't want to go through anything. We want to go through life on a flowery bed of ease, but the truth is that as Christians, we are going to have to endure. I realize that what I went through – all the pain and suffering – was not about me, but so I could encourage someone else that they can make it. If I never went through the storm and the fire, I would not be able to tell you that God is able to bring you out. There are many hurting people in the world that need to hear from real and transparent people. Nobody wants to hear from the super-Christians who have never been through anything; they've been saved all their lives. People need realness in this day and age; they need to see people who are in this world, but not of this world. Who have gone through heartbreaks, disappointments, fights with giants, issues, and cried many nights over broken dreams. They went through all of this, but they never quit, they never gave up.

They didn't end up in South Oaks (a mental institution); they didn't commit suicide – thought about it many times, but did not do it.

But now thus saith the Lord that created thee, O Jacob, and he that formed thee, O Israel, fear not: for I have redeemed thee, I have called thee by thy name; thou art mine. When thou passest through the waters, I will be with thee; and through the rivers, they shall not overflow thee: when thou walkthrough the fire, thou shalt not be burned; neither shall the flame kindle upon thee. ~ Isaiah 43:1-2

God was there all the time. No matter what you have gone through, you made it because God was there. You are able to soar above your circumstances. Somebody reading this book has one more step and they are out of their fire and into their destiny! Somebody has one more tear to cry – you thought you cried your last tear, but you have one more good cry –

and you can wave bye bye to those giants in your life! You are ready to fly now.

R. Kelly says, “I used to think that I could not go on. And life was nothing but an awful song. But now I know the meaning of true love. I'm leaning on the everlasting arms. I believe I can fly.”

CHAPTER EIGHT

I made it on broken pieces

The adversaries of the Lord shall be broken to pieces ~ 1 Samuel 2:10

How many of us have looked back over our lives and realized it was only by God's grace that we made it through every obstacle, disappointment, failure, and storm? On this journey called life we are faced with difficult situations and challenges. Often during these struggles, we don't see how it is humanly possible to make it out victoriously. The enemy will speak to us and make us feel like this is it; it is our final chapter. We try everything, but it appears like everything that we try fails.

Life has a way of throwing us a curve ball and oftentimes we cry out, "Lord, why is there so much pain? Why me?" We question God on why we were diagnosed with cancer, or why we can't pay our bills. One question I personally asked God was why my son had to leave his earthly home for his heavenly home at the tender age of eighteen. I relied on my favorite passages of Scripture to help me to get through one of my greatest storms of my life:

> *I exhort you to be of good cheer for there shall be no loss of any man's life among you but of the ship ~ Acts 27:22*

> *But the centurion, willing to save Paul, kept them from their purpose; and commanded that they which could swim should cast themselves first into the sea and get to land: And the rest, some on boards, some on broken pieces of the ship. And it came to pass that they all escaped safe to land. ~ Acts 27:43-47*

Everyone faces storms in their life. Some storms are natural disasters such as tornadoes, hurricanes, or blizzards. Others are personals storms such as loss of a job, loss of a loved one, setbacks, or relationship problems. Unfortunately, they are all a part of this journey called life. Therefore, we understand that in this life we are going to face many storms. The question is not whether we are going to go through storms in life; the question is, as we cope with the storms in life, how can we be unstoppable despite the storms?

In the passage of Scripture, Paul is imprisoned and on his way to Rome to stand trial. Paul warns them that it is not safe to travel this time of the year, but they ignore his warnings and take the trip anyway. How many times in our lives have we refused to listen to sound counsel and decide we are grown and we do not have to listen to anyone? You have the mindset that you are going to do things your way. It's like when we were children, our parents told us not to touch the stove because it is hot, and we had to touch the stove and get burned to truly believe it. Often in life, God will tell us not to do something and we go against the will of God and find ourselves in a storm. How much grief and pain would we have saved ourselves if we had listened to the voice of God?

The sailors did not listen to Paul. After all, who did he think he was? He was just a prisoner! Many times in life, we go astray because we look at the package that is carrying the message. The men didn't listen to Paul, and consequently they sailed right into the worst storm of their lives. They tried everything to save the ship. When nothing worked, they started to throw everything they didn't need overboard. Many of us are traveling through life with excessive baggage. We picked this baggage up from every storm we ever went through in life. Although the ship was destroyed, the men all survived, albeit some on broken pieces.

In 2009, I went through one of the fiercest storms of my life. I lost my son. The devil told me I might as well throw in the towel because this storm was going to take me out. He told me that I had preached my last sermon. He also asked me how I could mentor young people when my own child was gone. My son had been the choir director, so I couldn't stand to hear the choir sing anymore. I couldn't bear to speak to any of my friends who still had their children. I was on the verge of cussing out the next person who said that he was in a better place. I did not want to hear one more person say he was in a better place. I was tired of it!

At the end of my rope, on April 17, 2009, I was going to end it all and meet my son in "that better place." I was standing alone in my sister's kitchen holding two bottles of high blood pressure pills. As I poured the contents of the bottles into my hand, I was crying hysterically and asking God why He didn't just take me instead of my son. I heard a small whisper saying, "If you do this, you will never see him again. You are not ready to go." On that day, I put those pills down and slowly began my long road to recovery.

It was not easy because I made a lot of permanent decisions while I was in a temporary place. I was broken, but not destroyed. I might have been wounded, but I made it. You can still see the scars, but I made it. Many nights in the midnight hour, I have cried all night long asking God why I endured so much pain. I have not always been perfect, but I have been faithful.

There are some things that I have endured in my life such as physical, mental, and verbal abuse as a child; the loss of my child; and a failed marriage. Many people would never have made it through these storms because it would have killed them. They should have killed me, but thank God, I made it! I realized that per man, I should not still be here; I should have never made it through the harsh storms of life, but God had a plan for my life and my destiny was waiting for me.

I remember telling God I wanted to be anointed, not really knowing that the anointing was going to cost me something. God asked me how bad did I want it, and if I wanted it bad enough to weather the storms that were going to come. I made it through the storm unstoppable, but on broken pieces.

The one lesson I have learned is that not everyone wants you to make it out of your storm. Through much pain, I have discovered that you cannot share your dreams with everyone. There are going to be times in your life when you must plant your dreams in secret and water them with your tears in the midnight hour. There are people who have been placed in your life to be dream killers and they do not want you to survive your storm. They are waiting and watching for you to drown in your storms.

After the death of my son, my friends and even my family thought I was not going to make it through this storm. I was on a sabbatical from preaching because I did not want to preach from a place of hurt and anguish. I remember I attended a women's conference and the prophet prophesied to me, telling me God said I was going to make it. Not only was I going to make it out of this storm, but I was not going to look like what I been through. The fire was not meant to consume me, but to refine me. The prophecy continued with the Lord saying I was coming out of this storm blessed, coming out healed, coming out with more than I had at the beginning of the storm. I realized I am unstoppable!

The devil tried to stop me, but he realized he had to bring out his best artillery to stop my destiny. I learned that the greater the anointing, the harsher the storm. The storm set me free from conformability. The storm set me free from people and wondering what they thought about me. There were some things that were holding me back and it took the storm to set me free. The truth is that there was some stuff I didn't want to get rid of, but it took the storm to get it out of me for me to truly be unstoppable. While I was in the storm, I realized that if I was going to go where I have never been before, I would have to do what I have never done before.

I thank you, devil, because you propelled me into my destiny and while I was in my storm, I perfected my praise and my dance. God will use our storms as a vehicle to benefit others around us. Our trials and tribulations help to develop and confirm our testimonies. How can I tell you that you can make it through a storm if I have never been through a storm and made it myself?

Somebody reading this book is going through a storm and your ship has been destroyed. Despite this, don’t give up. You are unstoppable! You will make it through the storm. I can see something floating in the water. It’s a board. Further down, I can see a broken piece of a ship. Don’t give up! Grab hold of it and float to land! You have been through a storm, but you made it. It should have killed you. It should have killed me, but praise God, we are unstoppable! We made it on broken pieces, but we made it! Now it's time to step into our destiny. We are unstoppable!

CHAPTER NINE

It's delivery time

So shall my word be that goeth forth out of my mouth: it shall not return unto me void, but it shall accomplish that which I please, and it shall prosper in the thing whereto I sent it. ~ Isaiah 55:11

The process of giving birth is very long and painful. Natural childbirth can be long, painful, and even dangerous, but what I am talking about in this chapter is giving birth to the promises of God. In this season, we will give birth to those things that God promised us and those things that we have prayed for. We thought it was over, but it is not over. This is it – all the things that you have been waiting for.

We speak against everything that comes to abort your baby. Before you were born, while you were still in your mother's womb, God knew all about you. He knew your mistakes and your failures. He knew all about you and He still chose you. Those God-driven dreams are those dreams that, no matter how many miscarriages and abortions and stillborns you have experienced, those dreams must be born. It is during this time that you will discover the purpose for your pain, and you will turn your pain into your passion. Whereas natural birth starts with conception, spiritual birth begins with a vision. God has a purpose and a plan for our lives.

> *For I know the thoughts that I think toward you, saith the Lord, thoughts of peace, and not of evil, to give you an expected end. Then shall ye call upon me, and ye shall go and pray unto me, and I will hearken unto you. ~ Jeremiah 29:11-12*

We have many plans for our lives based on the promises of God. The promises of God in our life are sure no matter what it looks like. And no matter how many times you have lost a baby, you will give birth to God's promises. The process is not easy, but do not abort your dreams because the labor gets hard; make up your mind that this time your baby will be born. God will birth a new thing in you; when God has a calling on your life, you will give birth to your destiny, dreams, and aspirations. Many of us have been waiting for many years for the promises of God to be manifested in our lives, but it was a process. We had to deal with the issues in our lives and kill some giants before we could give birth to our promise. You must be delivered from your fears and your past.

What are your dreams? Do you want to finish your education, write a book, lose weight, or get a promotion at work? Whatever it is, if your mind can conceive it, your heart can believe it, then you can achieve it.

Birthing takes action. You have to push. You cannot just lie there and do nothing. In order to give birth, you have to push. If you want to stop having miscarriages you must set small, measurable, and obtainable goals. You have to write down your dreams and then wait on them.

> *And the Lord answered me, and said, Write the vision, and make it plain upon tables, that he may run that readeth it. For the vision is yet for an appointed time, but at the end it shall speak, and not lie: though it tarry, wait for it; because it will surely come, it will not tarry. ~ Habakkuk 2:2-3*

It has been a long painful process. You lost some things during your pregnancy. You lost some people, places, and things, but everyone cannot go with you to your destiny. So, do not make permanent decisions while you are in a temporary state. Don't try to rush childbirth; it will only end in more pain.

While I was in the waiting room, I got married to a man that was not part of my destiny. The enemy wanted to destroy me, so he send me package that was pretty on the outside, but on the inside was death and destruction.

Life is not always fair and things happen in your life that will send you in the opposite direction that you were headed in. But when you have a God-given dream, there is something inside of each of us that tells us that we are destined for more than we presently see. You need to know that where you are now is not your stopping place, but your birthing place. When you are pregnant with destiny, you are no longer satisfied with the status quo. You are no longer able to be managed and manipulated to stay in the circumstances that your dream finds you in. Your dreams will always move you toward a greater tomorrow.

Where there is no vision, the people perish: but he that keepeth the law, happy is he. ~ Proverbs 20:18

Joseph had a dream of promotion and elevation and he was extremely excited. But not everyone was excited; he was surrounded by the wrong midwives. Show me a person who cannot celebrate with a dreamer, and I will show you a person without a dream. Like Joseph, we expect those with no dreams to get excited about our dreams. While you were in the delivery room, you got so excited that your baby was finally coming that you wanted to run and tell somebody, and you thought they were going to be excited about the birth, but they were mad that you were still pregnant with your promise.

In order to birth your dreams, you have to forget the pain of your past miscarriage. But the process was worth it and now it is time to be wheeled into the delivery room. We are in the delivery room now and it's time to give birth to your dreams. You have been through spiritual miscarriage and abortions, but this time you carried the baby full term and it is time to push. Some of you are destined for greatness because you have experienced great pains in life. You survived your waiting period because, like in natural birth, we cannot hurry the process or the baby will be born prematurely. But you made up your mind that you are not going to leave this earth without giving birth to those visions, dreams, and aspirations that you have in your womb.

This time you have surrounded yourselves with midwives that are here to help you give birth, not kill your babies. They are going to tell you when to breathe and when to push. You see the old midwives that you hate are still wondering how you made it; how you did not lose your mind; how you could get out of bed day after day, after crying all night long. But you made it this time.

Don't give up now! You are a couple of pushes from your destiny. You are now facing the harder part and the pain is so intense, but don't give up. It's time to push. Push out every promise that God gave you. You might be in pain, but the pain will be worth it.

While you are in labor, don't think about the pain. Think about the dreams, visions, and aspirations that you are about to give birth to. This time, you did not let your dreams die. You did not give up on your dreams. So push, push, push! You are about to give birth to your dreams and visions – you are about to recover it all.

CHAPTER TEN

You shall recover it all

And David enquired at the Lord, saying, Shall I pursue after this troop? shall I overtake them? And he answered him, Pursue: for thou shalt surely overtake them, and without fail recover all. ~ 1 Samuel 30:8

[1] *And it came to pass, when David and his men*
were come to Ziklag on the third day, that the
Amalekites had invaded the south, and Ziklag, and
smitten Ziklag, and burned it with fire;
[2] *And had taken the women captives, that were*
therein: they slew not any, either great or small,
but carried them away, and went on their way.
[3] *So David and his men came to the city, and,*
behold, it was burned with fire; and their wives,

and their sons, and their daughters, were taken captives.

4 *Then David and the people that were with him lifted up their voice and wept, until they had no more power to weep.*

5 *And David's two wives were taken captives, Ahinoam the Jezreelitess, and Abigail the wife of Nabal the Carmelite.*

6 *And David was greatly distressed; for the people spake of stoning him, because the soul of all the people was grieved, every man for his sons and for his daughters: but David encouraged himself in the Lord his God.*

7 *And David said to Abiathar the priest, Ahimelech's son, I pray thee, bring me hither the ephod. And Abiathar brought thither the ephod to David.*

8 *And David enquired at the Lord, saying, Shall I pursue after this troop? shall I overtake them? And he answered him, Pursue: for thou shalt*

surely overtake them, and without fail recover all. (1 Samuel 30:1-8)

In this passage of Scripture, David and his men return from battle and they find their homes burned down and all of their women and children taken captive. David had been on a long journey. He was running from Saul who was trying to kill him, and he had just gotten out of yet another battle with the Philistines. And we know how the Philistines felt about David; they had a vendetta against him. He was the one that had killed their giant, Goliath, so you know that David was marked for assassination.

David and his men were tired from battle and they just wanted to go home. We can all relate to that. After a long day, we just want to go home. Many a day, after tying shoes, wiping noses, and reading the same story one hundred times, I just want to go home and rest. So, David was just excited to be on his way home, but when he got home, oh what distress and heartache he feels when, as soon as he got to the camp, he was met with the news that the Amalekites had burned the camp down. Not only had they burned down the camp, but they were now holding all the women and children hostage. Come on, now – we can deal with our house being burned down, but now you have messed with my family? Sometimes in life, we must deal with a double whammy, but David could still see the hand of the Lord still working in all of it.

We must learn how to find God in all situations, no matter what it looks like and no matter what it feels like. David had to say, "I have been down and out before and my God was there for me." He said, "The same God that was there when I slew the giant, and the same God that was there for the bear and the lion, that same God is going to help me today. I lost everything that I had, but I know that God is with me." If we really look at the test, we can see now God was still in control.

In verse two, it says that they did not kill any of them. They could have really lost it all, but it was not dead; it was just being held captive. That is what is happening to a lot of your stuff – the devil could not kill it, so he is just holding it hostage. The enemy took advantage of the fact that David and the men were not there, so they went and stole their stuff.

We continue to cry and to ponder over the stuff, but our stuff is not lost; it is just being held captive. We cry and weep over those things that we say the devil stole from us, but I have a little secret for some of you – the devil didn't steal your stuff, but while you were in the waiting room, you gave it to him. Some of your children are not acting right; they are out there on drugs, but they are not dead, they are just being held captive. Your money is not lost, but it is being held captive. Your dreams, visions, and aspirations are not dead, they were just being held captive. It is time for you to stop crying over your situation because it is not dead, it is just being held captive.

The first thing that you have to take back from the enemy is your faith – the faith that you will be able to recover it all. Faith is the evidence of things hoped for, but not yet seen. You have to envision yourself enjoying your stuff again. It is encouraging to know that our situations and circumstances are not dead, but they are being held captive. You shall recover it all.

But let's keep looking at David, our giant-slayer. He was fighting a giant in his waiting room and in the recovery room, he is still fighting. But let's look at David the day he discovered that his stuff was missing. In verse four, we find David having a pity party like most of us. We weep and cry, "Woe is me. Why me? Why did they take my stuff?" It is okay to cry. It is not true that big girls don't cry, because we do cry. So go ahead and get it out. Have one good cry, but don't wallow in it. Don't cry over the same things day after day. You should not still be crying over things that you lost five years ago. You got a divorce ten years ago and you are still saying all men are dogs? You have to get over it; in order to get it back, you have to get over the pain and the hurt.

Let's look at David. He was greatly distressed, for the people were talking about stoning him. Look what happened – those same people that were celebrating him yesterday turned on him, and today they wanted to kill him. This lets us know that we should not get discouraged when people turn on us because people will turn their back on you when things get rough. As great a leader as David was, the men still turned on him in times of sorrow. At that time, nobody remembered how many battles David had won. Not one person thought that David was the same man that killed the giant.

So as leaders, we have to stop going home and crawling under a rock when the people get distressed and want to stone you. If you are a supervisor of a job, don't be surprised and hurt when the people talk about you in the break room. That's how people are. They will set you up on a pedestal one minute, and bring you down just as quick or quicker.

But what did David do? He encouraged himself. There will be times in your life when you will have to encourage yourself. You have to pick yourself up and pat yourself on the back. You cannot wait for the flowers or the hallmark card. You have to stand up and be a man or woman of God.

I am more than a conqueror through Christ Jesus. I am the head and not the tail. I am blessed coming in and going out. God is about to turn it around for me. This is it. The devil cannot mess with my mind anymore. He can't have my stuff.

You have to encourage yourself. Is anybody ready to encourage themselves now? You have been through hell and high water, but you are still here and you are still standing. What you went through would have killed the average Joe, but you made it. So, after we encourage ourselves, then we go to our source in prayer and we ask God to help us make it through the night.

David went to God in prayer and David said, “God should I go after my stuff? Is it my time to get my stuff back?” And God answered him, “Pursue, for you shall surely recover it all.”

There comes a time in your life when you have to go boldly to the throne of grace. Those ‘now you lay me down to sleep’ watered-down prayers are not going to work. Somebody reading this right now should be praising God because you shall get back all of your stuff! God said it and I believe it. I don’t have to call no psychic hotline. I am standing on the Word of God that says I will recover it all. God said you can have your stuff back. The devil cannot hold your dreams, visions, and aspirations anymore.

You got happy about the vision, but you don’t want to step out on faith. God told David to pursue, to go after it. Many of us want our stuff back, but we don't want to move from our comfort zone where we are now. You have to leave your place of familiarity to go and get your stuff back. Even though our stuff is burned up where we are, we don't want to move to the place God is calling us to. God is calling us to a higher level. Our stuff is not here. It is at the next level. We would rather stay than to fight a battle that is already won. Is there anybody reading this book that is ready to go and get back their stuff? It is time to go and get back your stuff.

David took off to get his stuff back, but we see there is still trouble in the camp. Some of the men that started out with David were so weak from the previous battle, and after coming home to find their families gone, they quit because they could not go on. Don't get discouraged when you lose people while you are on your journey to get your stuff back. Not everybody will make it with you to your next level. Don't try to pull them along. Let them go. David did not get discouraged because he was not relying on those men to win the battle. God had already told him that he was going to recover it all.

So are you really ready to go and get your stuff back? You can have your joy back, your dreams and aspirations. You have recovered it all. Get up and praise God for whatever He has promised you. You can have it. If you want to go back to school, start applying to college right now. It doesn't matter what time it is. You can go online. If you want to start a business, start writing your business plan right now. If you want to write a book, get out your pen and paper and start writing.

It has been a long journey, but we made it. I started this journey on February 15, 2009 when I entered my waiting room. At that time, I did not even know what I was waiting for. All I knew was that I was experiencing the worst pain of my life and I really did not think I was going to make it out alive. I survived depression and suicidal thoughts. During the day, I wore a mask of joy, but at night I cried myself to sleep every night in my waiting room, constantly visited by demons that told me to give up, that I would never make it out. Then one day, I found myself being called out of my waiting room into the delivery room where I had to deal with those issues and strongholds in my life. And then I found myself in the recovery room, recovering from the many operations that I needed to purge myself of all those dead issues and I began to recover it all.

All my life I had dreamed of being a writer. I started many books, not to finish any. But now I have a story to tell that will empower other people that they can make it through the storm. I survived one major storm after another, but now some of my cloudy days are over.

Some of you are still in your waiting room. Wait on God. He will bring you out. He can deliver you from any issue and restore you back to a place in Him. It is time for you to walk into your destiny.

ACKNOWLEDGMENTS

I would like to thank my Lord and Savior Jesus Christ to whom I owe all of my gifts and talents.

I would like to thank everyone who traveled this rough road with me as I went from my waiting room to the recovery room. To Sabria Moten, you will always be my why. You are an intelligent and pretty young woman.

Once again, I would like to thank my physical family: my brothers and sisters, Gloria, Allison, Kim, Darren, Samuel and Greg. To my mother Willie Mae Millner, thank you for always being there. To my uncle James and to my uncle M.C. who I thank more than he knows. *Sally Homes* is on the horizon – I am working on it now.

Once again, thank you to my church family, the Church of Jesus Christ our Lord, and Bishop William and Margie Billups, thank you for teaching me that holiness is right.

To Amityville Head Start: remember to always chase your dream. What God has done for me, he will do for you.

To Marks of Excellence: thank you for always believing in me.

To UNAYO, my home away from home: continue to invest in the children in North Amityville; they are our future. Remember that troubles don't last always, and God will never put more on you than you can bear.

I would like to thank my Aunt Rose Pernell Thomas who has always been there for me.

To my besties Desiree Session, Nidia Paulino, Gayle Foulke, and Erika Moore: you guys continue to chase your dreams. There is greatness in each one of you.

To my niece and nephews: God has greatness in store for each of you. So proud of Destenique as she enters into twelfth grade; she is going to take the world by storm.

And to my readers – as long as you continue to support me and God gives me grace, I will continue to write. Look out for my next fictional novel, He's no Choir Boy.

And to Sharnel Williams: Girl, you rock. Keep living your dream life.

www.ingramcontent.com/pod-product-compliance
Lightning Source LLC
LaVergne TN
LVHW051100080426
835508LV00019B/1981

* 9 7 8 0 9 9 7 2 6 6 8 9 4 *